CROWOOD EQUESTRIAN GUIDES

Basic Tack

Vanessa Britton

The Crowood Press

First published in 1994 by
The Crowood Press Ltd
Ramsbury, Marlborough
Wiltshire SN8 2HR

This impression 2002

British Library Cataloguing-in-Publication Data
A catalogue record for this book is available from the British Library.

ISBN 1 85223 800 3

Picture credits
All photographs by Vanessa Britton
Line drawings by Jacqueline Darnell

Acknowledgements
Many thanks to show producer Wendy King for allowing me to use her
horses as models for many of the photographs. Also to Christine
Dunnett for allowing me to raid her tack shop.

Throughout this book, 'he', 'him' and 'his' have been used as neutral
pronouns and as such refer to both males and females. The term
'horses' may include ponies, and vice versa.

Typeset by Dorwyn Ltd, Rowlands Castle, Hants

Printed and bound in Great Britain by Bookcraft, Midsomer Norton

CONTENTS • 3

As the popularity of riding increases each year, so does the availability of tack and equipment for the horse. With modern advances in design, the area is now more confusing than ever before: in years gone by you could buy a simple piece of tack without too much hassle, but now there is a wide range to choose from and selecting the correct item can often be very complicated.

To add to the confusion, horse equipment seems to attract many followers of fashion. One minute the trend is for bright-orange, rubber-covered reins, the next it is for white ones, when in fact the major consideration should be whether the item is suitable for the purpose intended.

Having selected the right piece, the next step is to make sure it is fitted correctly. This is something which has to be learned before you can get down to any serious riding, whether it be for pleasure or in competition. Fitting tack incorrectly can lead to all sorts of problems. If the horse is uncomfortable he will start to object to his rider's wishes and might even sustain physical injuries as a result.

The key to the successful use of tack is simplicity. The best policy is to use the least amount of tack that is needed, so knowing what items not to use, and why, is also important.

Horses are all too often spoilt in their early years by inexperienced trainers or careless riders. As a result, at some stage in their lives, many horses need a little more gentle persuasion to see things our way. We can often help them towards this, through the selective and sympathetic use of tack. However, it should be understood that we only persuade the horse to comply with our wishes by using certain articles; we never force the horse to obey.

Advice frequently given by well-meaning horseowners on the use of different items can often seem bewildering. The purpose of this book, therefore, is to guide you through the maze of major tack items and equipment. A concise description of the construction and fitting of the various tack items, together with an easily understood explanation of their purpose and usage, will lead you to a clear understanding of this otherwise confusing area of horsemanship.

To help keep this understanding of tack clear in your mind, you should always remember the following guidelines:

1. Select only the best-quality items for the purpose intended.
2. Ensure your horse's comfort by selecting and correctly fitting the most appropriate material.
3. Look after every item of tack you own to ensure longevity, safety and continued comfort.

There are three main reasons why you may find yourself looking to purchase articles of tack. Firstly, if you are a new owner you will need a saddle and bridle in order to ride your horse. Secondly, you may have to replace a piece of tack which has broken, or become old and unsafe. Lastly, you may wish to use another piece of tack on your horse which you do not already have.

Knowing you need an article of tack is only the beginning however, because in selecting the right items you will need to consider size, material, cost, quality and possibly colour.

WHERE TO BUY?

For those who have never had to purchase tack before, knowing where to shop is also a consideration.

You need to find a tack shop (also known as a saddlers) that has friendly, knowledgeable staff. Finding the right place to begin with will pay dividends later on, as you will be assured of getting sensible advice about your requirements and will not be in danger of getting palmed off with tack that is unsuitable.

Most new horseowners will know at least one person who could recommend a helpful saddlers and this is the best place to start. It is also a good idea to take such an experienced friend along with you. Most saddlers are very helpful and will go to great lengths to try to match your description with what they feel is the most suitable item. However, if you cannot tell them whether your horse is a cob or full-size, even the best of saddlers will have difficulty in meeting your needs.

With or without the recommendation of a friend, you should ensure the retailer you choose is a member of your national governing body for saddlery; in the United Kingdom this is the British Equestrian Trade Association (BETA). To guarantee the quality of items being sold you should look for the crest of the relevant craftsmen's guild, which in the UK is the Society of Master Saddlers. This should be displayed in a prominent place within the shop. Not only do such signs give you the reassurance that you will receive expert advice, they also guarantee the quality of workmanship that has gone into the tack being sold.

Tack can also be purchased at sales, although this is not to be recommended if you are a novice on your own. New items are often available and they may seem a 'good buy' compared to shop prices, but they are usually cheap only because they have some

Buying tack from sales can be a risky business, especially if you are a novice on your own.

fault. The inexperienced eye may well overlook such defects, resulting in the purchase of a piece of tack which is unsafe – and costly, because it will need to be replaced sooner rather than later.

SECOND-HAND TACK

You might think it is always better to buy new tack if you can afford it, but this is not necessarily true. Tack comes in degrees of quality and a used piece of quality tack is always preferable to an inferior new piece. Horse equipment is expensive, so having invested in good quality in the first place most people tend to look after it well. A piece of quality used tack, which has been well cleaned and looked after, may have many more years use in it than a newer piece that has been poorly made or neglected.

Reputable saddlers often take in second-hand tack to sell on and they are usually quite fussy about what they accept, so buying from them is normally quite safe. However, it is also possible to buy used items from sales, and from other saddlers who are not so fussy. Here you have no guarantee of quality and so should make absolutely sure of the usefulness and safety of any items before purchase.

WHAT TO LOOK FOR

Quality should be sought at all times and by going to a reputable saddler you will be assured of getting it. Buying tack of an inferior standard might save a few pounds initially, but it will prove expensive in the long run. Firstly you will have to replace it far more quickly and, secondly, if it were to snap while being used it could cause a nasty accident, which might result in you or your horse being injured. So the golden rule is *'it is quality that counts'*.

It takes knowledge to know what piece of tack is suitable for a given purpose, but it takes experience to be able to judge quality. Every tack shop should check the stock it sells, but sometimes things get overlooked so it is up to you to be on your guard.

When buying used tack check to make sure there are no cracks or hidden faults.

Checkpoints

Whenever you are looking to purchase an article of tack, whether new or second-hand, you should run through a mental check list:

1. Is the stitching secure? Make sure there are no threads which look as though they have already started to work loose or wear.
2. Is the metal stainless-steel or nickel? Nickel can bend and break.
3. Where was the tack made? Does it carry the appropriate national standards mark?
4. Is it the right size? Measure it, as labels often get mixed up so they are not necessarily reliable.
5. It is made of the right material? Do you want leather or synthetic tack?
6. Is it a quality piece? Has it been well made; does it have a recognized crest?
7. If it is a piece of used tack, has it been well-maintained? If it is leather is it soft and supple, without cracks; if it is synthetic is it free from flaws, fraying or tears?
8. Do you really need this piece of equipment? Remember, simplicity is the key.

Before any tack can be fitted, the horse has to be prepared for wearing it. If your horse is already accustomed to wearing tack, preparation will involve making sure that he is properly groomed and is fit and healthy.

GROOMING

The horse should be groomed before and after every ride. While you may not have the time to give your horse a thorough grooming before you ride, you should always ensure that any mud or dirt is removed from any area where tack is to be placed. This is usually your horse's head and back, and his legs if protective boots are being used.

The pressure of tack will cause the small particles of sand and grit present in mud to rub against the skin, making the horse's skin sore. The effect is similar to that of trying to dry yourself with a towel on the beach, when you are still covered in sand.

Always groom your horse before tacking up and after a ride.

While carrying out your horse's daily routine grooming, you should check his skin for any rashes, cuts or parasites, as these may cause tack to rub or irritate. This will in turn cause the horse pain and more serious problems such as saddle sores or girth galls might develop, which will put your horse out of action unnecessarily. Paying attention to such routine matters will ensure your horse's comfort at all times when ridden.

The stabled horse who is rugged in winter, will obviously be easier to prepare for riding than the horse at grass, who is caked in mud. However, even though a stabled horse may appear spotless, small bits of straw or shavings can work their way in to the coat, so make a point of brushing the horse off before putting on any tack.

The reason for brushing your horse off after a ride is to remove any dried sweat, both for your horse's comfort and in order to keep your tack as clean as possible. As with mud, putting tack on top of dried sweat will cause soreness. If the sweat has not dried on returning from a ride, it helps to rinse him off and then dry him, as waiting for sweat to dry can take ages, and is unnecessary.

PREPARING TACK AREAS

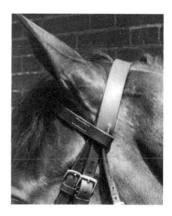

As well as being clean, in order to wear tack, the horse also needs to be made comfortable while tack is in use. This involves clipping and trimming certain areas. The area behind the horse's ears where the headpiece of the bridle sits is known as the bridle patch. Normally this is covered by the horse's mane, which often prevents the bridle from sitting comfortably, and securely. It is usual, therefore, to trim about 4–5cm (1¼–2in) of mane to allow the bridle to sit flat against the horse's skin.

The coarse 'cat hairs' (often seen on the clipped horse in spring), and possibly the horse's whiskers may also need trimming. The cat hairs grow out from between and around the horse's jaw bones. They often grow so long that they catch in the cheekpieces and noseband of the bridle, and as a result pinch the horse, so they are best removed as they serve no useful purpose.

It is important to trim a section of mane behind the horse's ears to allow the bridle to sit evenly and comfortably.

The trimming of a horse's whiskers is often discouraged as they serve to inform the horse when his mouth is close to an object and they also help to keep flies away from the horse's mouth and nostrils. However, having them caught in any tack used on the lower part of the horse's muzzle – such as a dropped noseband or a curb-chain – might prove more hazardous for the horse. So it is

It is sensible to remove the horse's whiskers from places where tack will be fitted, but do not remove them all.

sensible to remove the whiskers where the tack will sit, perhaps leaving those on the lower part of the horse's bottom lip for protection.

If exercise boots are to be used, the feathers on the back of the horse's legs might also need trimming.

THE CLIPPED HORSE

If you intend to clip your horse in the winter time, this will have a material effect on the sort of tack he should wear and the way in which it should be worn. Many people, especially hunting folk, used to give their horses a full clip, where the hair is completely removed from every part of the horse's body. Such a clip can cause problems with horses who have sensitive skin, and so the hunter clip (where the saddle patch is left on), is now preferred because the hair forms a cushion of protection between the horse's skin and the saddle.

The reason for clipping is to prevent the horse from sweating too much. As the girth area is prone to sweating, this is usually clipped off. For clipped horses with sensitive skin, it might be necessary to use a softer girth; a cotton one instead of a leather one, for example.

A hunter clip provides a cushion of protection between the horse's skin and the saddle.

If a horse's head is also clipped, you need to make absolutely sure that all parts of the bridle are lying flat against the skin. Without the protective layer of hair, any parts of the bridle that do not lie flat can rub together, pinching the skin in between.

HEALTH

The health of your horse will also dictate the type of tack you use. If your horse has a physical problem, such as a sore or wound, it may still be possible to ride him by using tack that is designed to protect such areas.

Obviously, a horse that is unwell should never be ridden, but there are also other health reasons for not riding a horse: an allergy or skin condition, for example, which will be made worse by the use of tack, will have to be cleared up first.

There are also conditions, such as ringworm, which are contagious and so it is sensible not to share tack between horses, even if they are all your own animals.

FITNESS

A horse that has been turned out for a rest will come up in what is known as a 'soft' state, which means that his flesh is flabby. Such horses are more prone to getting sores from tack, and so softer materials should be used until the horse is muscled up.

Rubbing surgical spirit or salt water into the back and girth areas also helps to harden the skin, although you should ensure that there are no cuts or grazes in the skin before doing this. These areas are more prone to sores because they take the pressure of tack in use.

As the horse is ridden and becomes fitter, he may also become stronger. It might be necessary, therefore, to use either stronger articles of tack, such as a stronger bit, or to add a piece of tack, such as a martingale. While many people would argue that you should be a capable enough rider to school your horse to a degree where you have enough control without the use of stronger tack, this theory is useless if your horse is so full of himself that he drags you off across the fields at the first opportunity.

Summary
1. Before the horse is tacked up you should ensure he is free from dirt or grease and that he is fit and healthy.
2. Tack should never be put on top of mud or dried sweat.
3. You should check your horse for any rashes, cuts or skin parasites before tacking up.
4. For your horse's comfort, and to ensure the tack sits safely on your horse, you may need to trim certain areas of mane or other hair.
5. Some horses have more sensitive skin than others, especially when they are clipped, so softer materials might be needed.
6. Ringworm is contagious, so it is not a good idea to share tack between horses.
7. Rubbing surgical spirit or salt water into 'soft' areas will help to harden the skin.
8. Generally, the fitter the horse the stronger he will become so other tack might be needed.

The purpose of any bridle is to provide the means of control over a horse's movement, which is achieved by giving the correct signals through the reins, coupled with other ridden aids.

While all bridles do primarily the same job, there are various types, each designed to be more suitable than another for a given purpose. However, there are three basic designs: the single bridle, which uses one bit; the double bridle, which uses two bits; and the bitless bridle, which uses no bit at all (*see* bitless bridles page 36). All bridles are variations on one or other of these designs.

THE SINGLE BRIDLE

The single bridle is correctly known as the **snaffle bridle**, although this does not mean that only a snaffle bit can be used. A single bridle consists of:

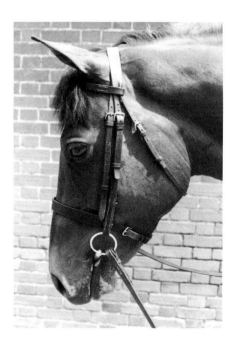

An ordinary snaffle bridle with cavesson noseband.

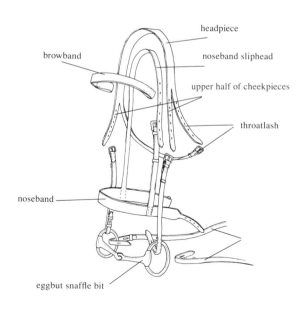

headpiece

browband

noseband sliphead

upper half of cheekpieces

throatlash

noseband

eggbut snaffle bit

Components of the snaffle bridle.

- A headpiece and throat-lash
- Two cheekpieces
- A browband
- A noseband
- A set of reins
- A bit

Assembly and Purpose

The **headpiece** and **throat-lash** are made from a single piece of leather. The purpose of this part of the bridle is to hold the cheek-pieces in place and, along with them, support the bit in the correct position. The throat-lash will not prevent the bridle from being pulled off the horse's head, but it will help to keep the bridle in place.

The two **cheekpieces** support the bit in the mouth. On each side, one end of the cheekpiece fixes to the bit and the other attaches to the headpiece.

The **browband** slips onto the headpiece, and holds it forward in place behind the horse's ears.

Nosebands come in various designs (*see* nosebands, page 19), but the cavesson is the standard type. The headstrap (slip-head) of the noseband slips through the browband and sits under the head-piece. It usually buckles on the near (left-hand) side of the horse.

The **reins** also come in various designs (*see* reins, page 33) and provide the means of communication between the rider's hands and the horse's mouth.

A plain **snaffle bit** (*see* bits, page 22) is most commonly used, and is the only bit suitable for beginner riders. It is held in position by the cheekpieces and the reins are attached below these.

THE DOUBLE BRIDLE

The double bridle is a complex system using two bits, a bridoon and a curb (*see* bits, page 22). In competent hands, a double offers precise control, but if used incorrectly it can cause much confusion and pain.

All the components of a single bridle are used in the double, and in addition, another cheekpiece – together with its own slip-head to hold the bridoon – and another set of reins for the curb bit are incorporated.

Components of the double bridle.

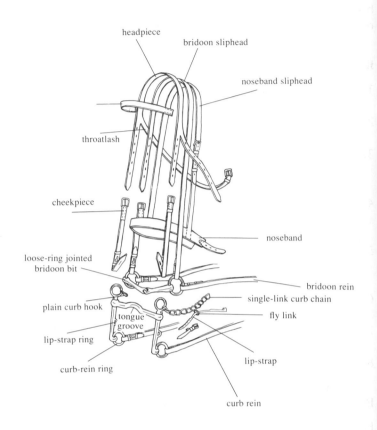

headpiece

bridoon sliphead

noseband sliphead

throatlash

cheekpiece

noseband

loose-ring jointed bridoon bit

bridoon rein

single-link curb chain

plain curb hook

fly link

tongue groove

lip-strap ring

curb-rein ring

lip-strap

curb rein

A double bridle.

In order to avoid too many buckles on the near side of the horse's head, the bridoon cheekpiece does up to its own slip-head on the off (right-hand) side, which slips through the browband and sits alongside the noseband's slip-head on the poll. The original cheekpieces hold the curb bit. The bridoon reins are always slightly wider than the curb reins to prevent confusion. A cavesson is the only noseband which should be used with a double bridle.

PUTTING ON A BRIDLE

There are two methods of putting on a bridle: one for the horse that stands quietly for bridling, and another for the horse that tries to lift his head away from you. In either case, before starting, ensure the noseband and throat-lash are unbuckled.

Bridling the Quiet Horse

1. Rest the rein buckle on the headpiece and hang the bridle on your left shoulder (browband away from you).
2. Stand on your horse's near side. Take hold of his headcollar and unclip the lead rope.
3. Place the reins over his head. Hold them together under his neck while removing the headcollar. Hang the headcollar up after removing otherwise you or your horse may trip up on it.
4. Take the bridle and hold the headpiece in your right hand. Let the bit rest on your left hand or vice versa, whichever feels easiest.
5. Bring the bit up to your horse's lips and insert your thumb into the corner of his mouth. This will encourage him to open his mouth.
6. When he does so, gently insert the bit while drawing the bridle up your horse's forehead.
7. Once the bit has been accepted, use your left hand to help pull the bridle gently over your horse's ears.
8. Fasten the noseband and throat-lash.

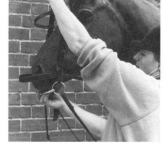

Putting the bridle on a horse who stands still.

Bridling the Horse that Lifts his Head

Follow steps 1–3 above, then:
4. Hold the bridle in your left hand. Put your right arm under your horse's jaw and around his head on the right side, and rest your hand mid-way up his face.
5. Take hold of the bridle cheekpieces in your right hand, while still resting it on his face, to prevent him from lifting his head.
6. Use your thumb to encourage him to open his mouth, guide in the bit whilst drawing the bridle up his forehead. Ensure you keep your hand resting on his face to discourage him from raising his head.
7. Follow steps 7 and 8 above.

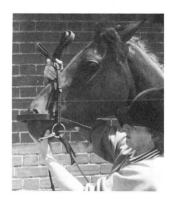

Bridling the horse who lifts his head.

Fitting

Once in place, the bridle needs to be adjusted for maximum safety and comfort.

Once the bit has been accepted, gently slip the bridle over his ears using both hands.

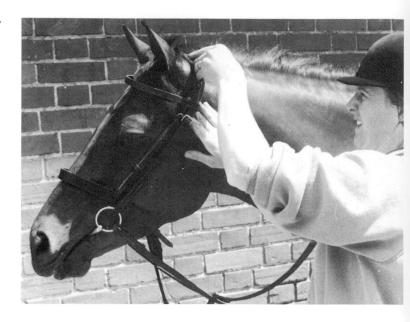

The cheekpieces   The position of the bit is altered by raising or lowering the cheekpieces. (*See* bits, page 22, for fitting of the various bits.)

The headpiece   This should lie evenly over the head with the cheekpieces buckled on even holes either side just above eye level.

The browband   This should sit low enough so as not to rub the base of the horse's ears. You should be able to slide a finger under it comfortably. If it is too long, it will allow the headpiece to slip back, and if too short it will pull the headpiece tight into the base of the ears, causing it to pinch and rub.

The throat-lash   Once buckled, this should allow a hand's width to be placed between it and the horse's jaw. If it is too tight it will restrict the windpipe when the horse flexes his head and neck.

The cavesson noseband   This should allow two fingers to be placed between it and the horse's jaw. It should lie about 2.5cm (1in) below the cheekbone. (For other types of noseband, *see* page 19.)

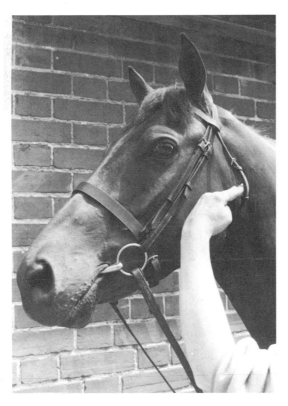

You should be able to place the width of your hand between the throat-lash and your horse's jaw.

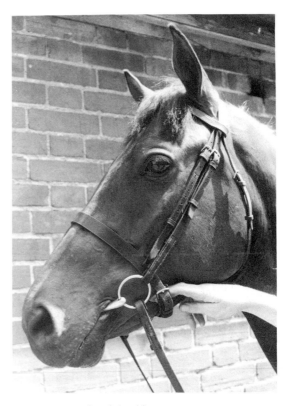

A cavesson noseband should allow the width of two fingers between it and the horse's jaw.

THE 'LOOK'

Leather bridles are finished in different ways, according to their intended purpose and the type of horse that will wear them.

The stout, plain bridle is mostly seen on large, heavyweight hunters and is useful for everyday and riding-school wear as it will withstand constant use.

Lighter, stitched bridles are used in show hack, riding horse and pony classes in order to show off a horse's 'good looks'.

A medium-weight bridle, which may or may not be stitched, is commonly used on dressage horses, small, lightweight or ladies' hunters, showjumpers and eventers.

'The Look'. Tack can be used to complement a horse's features. A quality hunter will carry a stout bridle well.

A lighter riding horse will look better in finer tack.

Rolled leather bridles used to be popular but seem to be less so nowadays.

Browbands are also used to create a certain 'look'. They can be stitched to match stitched bridles or they can be decorated with velvet, plastic or brass. Velvet ones are often used on show ponies to make them look pretty, while brass ones are traditional wear for stallions. Plastic ones are a poor relation to the velvet sort and soon start to split.

Event and cross-country riders also seem to like to have their tack and clothing colour co-ordinated and so have browbands, nose-bands, reins, boots and clothing all finished in the same colours.

Washable synthetic bridles are now also available and they are extremely good for everyday use because they cut in half the time required to clean them.

Most riders think of nosebands as a means of restraint. While this is to some extent true, their effect is dictated by the other tack, especially the bit, being used. The principal purpose of a noseband is to assist, and in some cases alter, the action of the bit.

TYPES OF NOSEBAND

The **cavesson** is the most commonly used noseband. It does not restrict the horse or the action of the bit, but does prevent the horse from opening and crossing his jawbones.

The front of a cavesson is sometimes covered in a dense roll of lamb's wool to prevent the horse from seeing things below him that may spook him, and to discourage him from throwing his head in the air, especially when approaching a jump.

The **drop noseband** is used to prevent the horse from evading the bit by opening his mouth or crossing his jaws, thus sliding the bit away from its correct position on the tongue and bars. A drop is also useful for a horse that tends to throw his head up violently. In this situation, a momentary increase of pressure upon the nasal passages will act as a slight restriction on breathing, which will in turn encourage the horse to lower his head.

A drop noseband should sit a hand's width above the nostrils, with the rear straps fastening below the bit. When fitted, there should be room for two fingers between the noseband and the horse's face.

The **flash** consists of a cavesson with a small loop sewn into the front of the nosepiece through which a longer, thinner strap passes, which fixes around the horse's muzzle below the bit. The cavesson part is fitted in the same way as an ordinary cavesson and the lower strap in the same way as a drop.

In effect, the flash is a cavesson which incorporates the action of a drop. It gives more control than the cavesson, but is less severe than the drop, because the point of pressure acting on the nasal bone is higher up above the bit, without the lower strap pushing the bit into the corners of the mouth. The flash is often used in preference to a drop, as a standing martingale can still be used on the cavesson part.

The **Grakle** has two loops of leather which sit comfortably through a flat round piece of leather, in a figure-of-eight design. One of the straps sits above the bit and one below. The two should cross on the front of the horse's nose at the point where the caves-

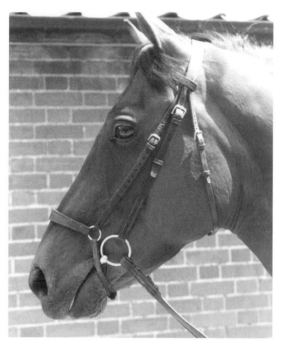

A drop noseband.

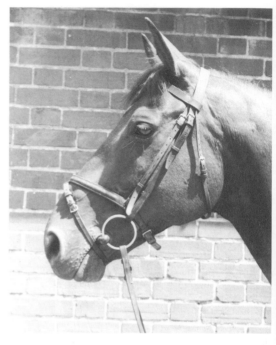

A flash noseband.

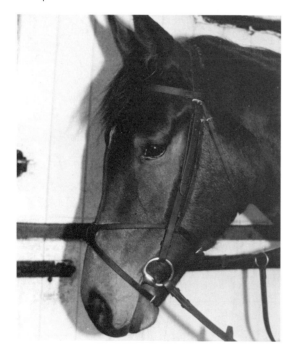

A Grakle noseband.

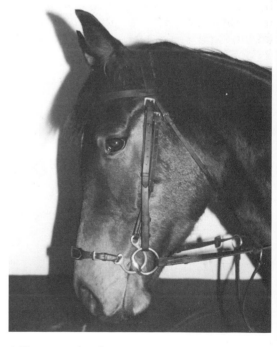

A Kineton noseband.

son usually sits. The two straps are fastened as tightly as the caves-son and the drop.

The Grakle is particularly suited to horses who constantly open their jaws and fight the bit. A gentle pressure is exerted on the muscles around the horse's cheeks, and the lower strap affords the same action as the flash.

The **Kineton** has two rounded metal loops which sit behind the mouthpiece of the bit, curving around the inside of the bit cheeks, with a metal reinforced nosepiece.

The metal loops do not come into force until pressure is applied to the rein. Pressure is applied to the nose and bit through the reins, forcing the horse to lower his head. The Kineton is useful for hard-pulling horses, as it can prevent the horse's mouth from being ruined by continuously pulling on the bit.

The **Australian cheeker** is made of a single piece of flat rubber, shaped in an upside-down 'Y' with flat discs at the end with holes in. A small headpiece loop attaches the noseband to the bridle. The discs are pulled over the bit rings, and the strap runs up the centre of the horse's face and fastens to the centre of the headpiece by a buckle. It is often used on racehorses, but can also be used as a remedial device to prevent the horse from putting his tongue over the bit, so preventing evasion.

PROBLEMS

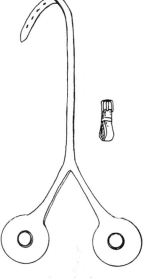

An Australian cheeker.

Most problems occur when nosebands are incorrectly fitted to individual horses. A common fault with many nosebands, especially cavessons, is that the nosepiece is too short and the rear too long, which makes for poor fitting. The slip-head then lies in front of the bridle cheekpieces, with the rear strap and buckle slipping lower than is desirable. Thus, the horse's skin is often pinched between the nosepiece and the bit cheeks, resulting in the horse's raising his head to try to alleviate the discomfort.

Drops, flashes and Grakles are often fitted too tightly and too low. Consequently the horse's breathing is interfered with and he is unable to relax his lower jaw. Nosebands are not intended to 'clamp' the horse's mouth shut. This causes the horse pain and he will naturally fight against the discomfort.

The nosepiece of a Kineton *must* sit above the end of the nasal bone. If it lies lower than this, it becomes a very cruel piece of equipment and its action far too severe to serve any purpose.

When selecting a suitable bit for a horse, the first considerations must be his comfort, and our safety. A bit needs to be the right size for his mouth and great care should be taken to ensure a correct fit. It is also important to choose the correct type of bit for the horse. Too strong, and he may rebel against it; too weak, and the rider may have a job to control him.

The action of any bit depends upon its design and on the horse's head position. We cannot use a certain type to achieve a certain head carriage, as this only comes through correct riding and schooling. We should also bear in mind that the other tack being used can alter the action of a bit.

In general, bits can be divided into three families: snaffles, curbs and pelhams.

SNAFFLES

While snaffles have a milder action than curb bits, there is a huge variety within the family, ranging from the very mild to the quite severe. The following factors determine the severity of a snaffle bit:

- The thickness of the mouthpiece. Thick mouthpieces are less severe than thinner ones.
- The design of the mouthpiece, whether mullen, which is unjointed and slightly curved, or jointed; the former is milder.
- The design of the rings, whether eggbutt or loose ring. Eggbutt rings are fixed to the mouthpiece and allow the horse less play on the mouthpiece than do loose rings.
- Whether the bit has cheekpieces or not; those with are milder.
- Bit materials. Common materials include metal (stainless steel), which is the hardest on the mouth; vulcanized rubber, which is less hard; and nathe and soft rubber which are the mildest.

Snaffle Mouthpieces

The snaffle family can be sub-divided into different categories. There are many variations on the mouthpiece and bit cheeks.

The **mullen mouthpiece**, whether of rubber or vulcanite, is the mildest of all, and a stainless steel one is only slightly stronger. It is designed to ease the pressure on the bars of the jaw (the gap in the teeth through which the mouthpiece passes), by putting more pressure on the tongue. It also acts on the corners of the lips.

A stainless steel mullen mouthpiece (top); and a single-jointed snaffle, which produces a nutcracker action (bottom). Both have eggbutt rings.

The **straight bar mouthpiece**, as the name suggests, is simply a straight bar, without a curve. It acts almost entirely on the tongue and corners of the lips.

The **single-jointed mouthpiece** produces a nutcracker action which puts more pressure on the bars of the mouth. It also acts on the roof of the mouth, the tongue (although less so than the straight bar); and on the corners of the lips.

The two sections of the bit, which meet at the joint in the centre, are called arms. It is preferable if these are slightly curved, and the joint linking the two fairly loose, but not to such an extent that the arms rotate.

There are a variety of rings and cheeks on single-jointed bits. The range includes flat ring, eggbutt, loose ring, D-ring, large ring, half-cheek, and full-cheek variations.

The **double-jointed mouthpiece** is designed to eliminate the nutcracker action by being joined in the centre by a middle link of some kind. It acts on the bars of the mouth and the lips.

The **ported mouthpiece** has a raised element in the centre of the mouthpiece. While the port has been a familiar part of the design of curb bits for many years, it has been less so on snaffles until recently. The ported mouthpiece is designed to remove pressure from the tongue by allowing the tongue to fill the port, which as a result enables the mouthpiece to achieve a greater contact with the bars of the mouth.

The **rollered mouthpiece** is designed to prevent the horse from grabbing hold of the mouthpiece. It is often seen on young horses as it encourages 'play'. Copper rollers spaced alternately with ordinary ones help a dry-mouthed horse to salivate.

Types of Snaffle

The most commonly used bit is the single-jointed eggbutt snaffle, and this is a good choice for beginner riders. However, there are other snaffles that are also in common use.

The **German snaffle** often has a hollow mouthpiece offering a light contact. Its mouthpiece is thick and therefore kind.

The **D-ring** has large D-shaped rings to stop the bit being pulled through the mouth. The arms are often quite thin, making for a fairly strong bit.

The **French link** is a double-jointed bit, with a centre link joining the two arms. The link is peanut-shell shaped and lies flat, making it a comfortable and fairly mild bit. Many horses who have rejected other types of snaffle will settle in a French link.

The **Fulmer** is a fairly mild bit. It has full cheeks which prevent the

German snaffle (top); eggbutt snaffle with thicker mouthpiece (bottom). Both are very kind bits, although any bit is only as mild as the hands on the other end of the reins.

bit from being pulled through the horse's mouth and is often used on young, un-schooled horses to help keep them straight. Sometimes they are fixed to the bridle by little keepers, to prevent play. They can be single- or double-jointed.

The **Dr Bristol** is a double-jointed bit, and unlike the French link, the middle plate lies at an angle to the tongue unless the horse's head carriage is in the desired position, when it will lie flat. Thus it is more severe than the French link. However, many horses go well in one with good results, when other bits have proved unsuitable.

The **Dick Christian** is a sensitive, double-jointed bit. Instead of the usual flat plate, it employs a central ring to join the two arms. It is ideal for horses with sensitive mouths.

The **twisted snaffle** is often used on horses that pull in the hope that the severity will stop the horse. This is unfortunate because this bit can inflict great pain, especially in the

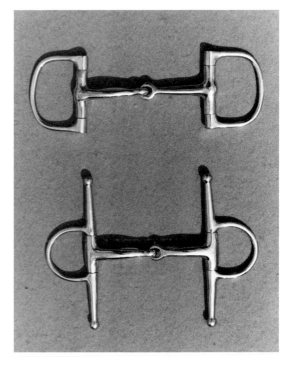

D-ring snaffle (top); Fulmer snaffle (bottom).

French link (top); Dr Bristol (bottom) – note the angled centre plate.

Fillis snaffle (top), one of the few snaffles that incorporate a port to provide more room for the tongue; twisted snaffle (bottom).

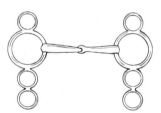

Belgian snaffle.

A gag snaffle fitted to an ordinary bridle with cavesson noseband.

hands of the inexperienced, and as a result it defeats the object in that the horse just pulls all the more in an attempt to run away from the pain.

The **Belgian snaffle** has become very popular, especially with showjumpers and eventers. It has three rings, thus offering a choice of rein position. Although it is called a snaffle, it does provide leverage. When the rein is attached to the lower ring, a curb action is produced. Ideally two reins should be used to allow a more subtle action. It can be fairly mild or more severe, depending on where the rein is attached. In competent hands, this bit can be used to good effect.

The **gag snaffle** is often used as a means of controlling a strong horse. It has holes in the bit rings, through which specially adapted cheekpieces pass, which then attach to the reins, thus allowing an upward movement of the bit in the mouth. There are quite a few types of gag, and while often only one rein is used, it is far preferable to use two: one, as described above, which is attached via the bit to the cheekpiece and which produces the severe gag action; and the other on the cheek ring, independent of the gag. In this way, the more severe action need only be brought into play when necessary. The action of the gag acts strongly upon the corners of the mouth, and also applies pressure to the poll.

Bridoon

A bridoon is the snaffle part of a double bridle. In effect, a bridoon is a scaled-down version of an ordinary snaffle: the rings are much smaller and as a result the action is more direct. The mouthpiece is also slimmer, in order to allow for the curb bit in the mouth as well. Both the bridoon and the curb are controlled independently. When handled correctly, the bridoon raises the horse's head and the curb produces the desired flexion.

CURBS

There are many curb bits to choose from and although they all look very severe, in the right hands some can be quite mild. The most common curb bits are the various Weymouth designs, which are those most commonly used with a double bridle.

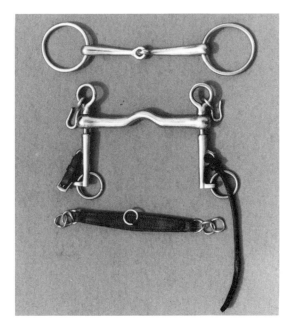

The two bits used with a double bridle: a bridoon (top); and a sliding-cheek Weymouth together with a leather curb-chain (bottom).

The curb mouthpiece usually has a tongue groove in the centre to ensure comfort. Curbs should always be used with a curb-chain and lip-strap. The curb-chain, which can be fitted with a rubber or leather cover for horses that object to the feel of the chain, attaches to hooks fixed to the upper rings of the curb bit. A round 'fly link' is attached to the middle of the chain, through which the lip-strap passes.

The lip-strap has a short buckle which fixes to the nearside 'D' on the curb bit, and a longer strap which passes from the off-side 'D', along the lip groove, through the fly link, and attaches, fairly loosely, to the short buckle.

Curb bits are used on their own but do tend to make the horse over bend, as the action of the snaffle – to raise the horse's head – is missing. The purpose of a curb bit is to produce a degree of flexion by applying pressure to the chin groove through the curb-chain, and to the poll through the leverage afforded by the cheekpieces.

The longer the cheeks on a Weymouth the more severe the action. The **Tom Thumb Weymouth** has a thick mouthpiece and only short cheekpieces so is the mildest of all Weymouths.

The **German dressage Weymouth** produces excellent results. The

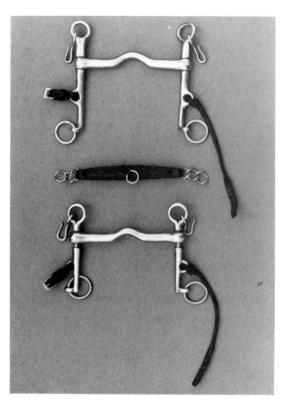

A fixed-cheek Weymouth (top); a sliding-cheek Weymouth (bottom).

mouthpiece is hollow, usually with a port, and the cheeks are fixed. The cheekpieces are of medium length. Used correctly, this is a kind bit, especially useful for occasions when double bridles are compulsory wear.

The **sliding-cheek Weymouth** is the most common type of curb used on a double bridle. The slide movement, which is usually 13mm (½in) but can be more, together with the cheekpiece length, will govern its severity.

Curbs should be used only by experienced riders because their action is complex. They act on the bars, the tongue, the roof of the mouth (with greater severity as the size of the port increases), the chin groove (via the curb-chain), and they also apply indirect pressure to the poll. Needless to say, a heavy-handed rider could cause a lot of damage to the horse's mouth.

PELHAMS

Pelhams employ only one mouthpiece, and are used as an alternative to a double bridle. The idea is to try to combine the effects of the two bits used with a double. However, the action of a pelham is imprecise and when used with roundings instead of two reins, the action is even more vague. The curb-chain is also likely to slide up the horse's jaw, which can cause further confusion. Nevertheless, it does have its uses and some horses go very well in one, treating it with more respect than a snaffle.

There are variations, mainly in types of cheek (longer or shorter) and mouthpieces (jointed or mullen, metal or vulcanite for example), and there is also the **Kimblewick** which is a modified design. To look at a Kimblewick you might describe it as an eggbutt D-ring snaffle with a curb-chain fitted. It is a single-rein Pelham, without the lower cheek section. As a result it has a modified Pelham action, without as much leverage. It too may have various mouthpiece designs.

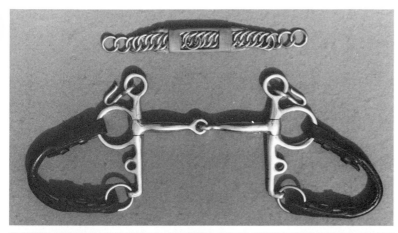

Jointed Pelham with roundings attached and a curb-chain with rubber guard, useful for a sensitive horse.

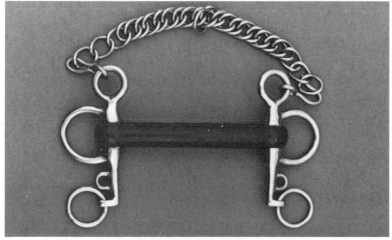

Mullen-mouth vulcanite Pelham.

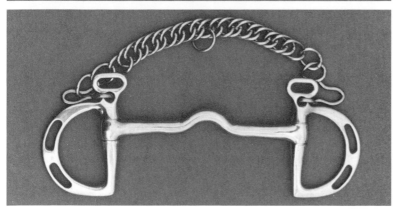

Kimblewick with two rein positions.

THE HORSE'S MOUTH AND HEAD

A bit acts on the horse's mouth and head in various ways, depending on the type being used.

The corners of the mouth When you put pressure on the reins, you can immediately see the bit acting on the corners of the mouth. Slight pressure will cause the corner to wrinkle a little. Pulling too hard will cause more wrinkling and will pull the lips taut, which is likely to cause sores or even tears.

The tongue The tongue always receives pressure from the bit when in use, regardless of the type used.

The bars The bars of a horse's mouth are the areas of toothless gum, between the front teeth (incisors) and the back teeth (molars). The bit should always rest on the bars, so that it does not bang against any teeth.
   Tushes are small pointed teeth which lie behind the incisors in both top and bottom jaw. They are usually seen only in male horses, although some mares do have them. It is important to check that the bit does not come into contact with the tushes.

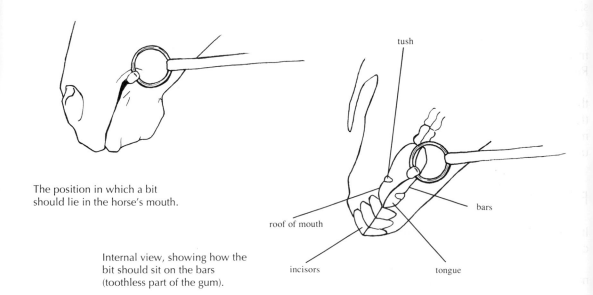

The position in which a bit should lie in the horse's mouth.

Internal view, showing how the bit should sit on the bars (toothless part of the gum).

tush

roof of mouth

bars

incisors

tongue

The roof of the mouth   The bit comes into contact with the roof of the mouth when the mouth is closed, especially when a bit with a port is used.

The nose   The nose receives pressure from the bit indirectly, through the noseband. Pressure on the bit makes the horse react in his jaw, which brings the action of the noseband into play.

The poll   Again, the poll receives pressure indirectly from the bit, through the headpiece, especially from the leverage of a curb bit or the action of a gag.

Chin groove   This receives pressure only if a curb-chain is used.

CORRECT SIZE

A bit is the correct size if about 5mm (¼in) of the mouthpiece can be seen either side of the horse's mouth. To check this with a jointed bit, you should pull it out straight while fitted in the horse's mouth. Your two index fingers should sit snugly between the bit rings and the mouth.

Every horse should have his mouth measured to determine the size of bit required as it is not possible to generalize on suitable sizes. It is the size of the horse's jaw that determines the width required, not the size of the horse or pony itself.

To measure for bit size, hold a piece of baling twine in the horse's mouth, and pull it tight between the bars, to the corners of the lips. Remove and measure the length; then add on 1cm (⅜in).

As a rough guide, most horses and ponies can be fitted with a bit that falls in a range of between 10cm (for a small pony) and 15cm (for a larger riding horse). Also bear in mind that while a thin mouthpiece is usually more severe, a very thick mouthpiece will be uncomfortable for a pony with a particularly small mouth.

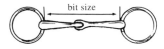

A bit's size is determined by the size of its mouthpiece.

FITTING

It is essential to fit the bit properly if it is to offer maximum effect and comfort.

A jointed snaffle should sit snugly into the corners of the mouth making a very slight wrinkle.

A straight mouthpiece should sit into the corners of the mouth, but should not wrinkle the lips.

The bits on a double bridle are fitted slightly differently. The bridoon is slightly higher in the mouth than a normal snaffle, where a definite wrinkle can be seen. The curb is suspended about 2.5cm (1in) below this to prevent the bits' crossing over when in use and to help keep the curb-chain in the chin groove. The curb-chain should be twisted until the links all lie flat against the groove before placing the last link over the hook (ensure that the chain remains flat after attaching it); the lip-strap should be fitted fairly loosely.

PROBLEMS CAUSED BY BAD BITTING

Mistakes are easily made when selecting and fitting bits. The most common problems include:

- Too narrow a bit: this will pinch the corners of the mouth.
- Too wide a bit: this could slip from side to side causing soreness. If too wide a jointed snaffle is used, the joint will lie too low in the mouth, allowing the horse to put his tongue over the bit.
- Too thin a bit: this may prove to be too severe as all the pressure is concentrated on a small area.
- Too thick a bit: this might cause too much tongue pressure on a shallow-mouthed horse.
- A bit fitted too high in the mouth: this can pinch and rub the corners of the mouth and come into contact with the molars.
- A bit fitted too low in the mouth: this will allow the tongue to come over the bit; a jointed type might bang against the incisors.

If you feel confident that your selection is a good one, and that the bit is correctly fitted, and yet your horse does not seem happy, you should look elsewhere for a solution. While the problem might seem to originate from the bit, the cause may actually lie elsewhere: a sore mouth or insensitive riding, for example.

Horses should have their teeth checked annually for sharpness and other problems, either by a trained equine dentist or a veterinary surgeon. A horse with a sore mouth will not go well in any bit and we should not expect him to.

If, having considered all the possibilities, you still have problems in finding a bit that your horse goes well in, you should seek advice from an expert before too much damage occurs.

Horses should have their teeth checked annually for sharpness and other problems.

All reins serve the same purpose: to provide contact with the bit through the rider's hands, yet there are certain things which, in the interests of safety and effectiveness, need to be considered when choosing a suitable pair. The wrong choice can lead to less sensitive communication between the rider's hands and the horse's mouth and can, therefore, cause problems when riding.

WIDTH

Firstly the size of your hands needs to be considered. An average pair of reins is usually between 1.5cm (⅝in) and 2cm (¾in) wide. Too wide for your hands and the reins will be uncomfortable, as well as harder for you to control sensitively; too narrow and you will be clenching your hands in order to keep a grip on them. Generally the rule is the smaller the hand the narrower the rein.

LENGTH

Another consideration is the length of the reins. Most reins are between 132cm (52in) and 152.5cm (60in) in length, although pony reins are usually between 122cm (48in) and 137cm (54in).

Reins that are too short are restrictive and potentially dangerous; reins that are too long are hazardous as they provide an opportunity for the foot to get caught in the loop.

The length of rein required is determined by the length of the horse's neck. Ideally the rein length from bit to rein buckle should be 28cm (11in) greater than the length of the horse's neck measuring from withers to mouth.

TYPES OF REIN

Rubber-covered reins   These seem to be the most popular as they provide a good grip in all weather conditions.

Plain leather   These are usual for showing. However, for normal riding use they are not very practical or safe as they quickly become slippery when wet.

Plaited leather   These are plain leather at the bit end. About 25cm

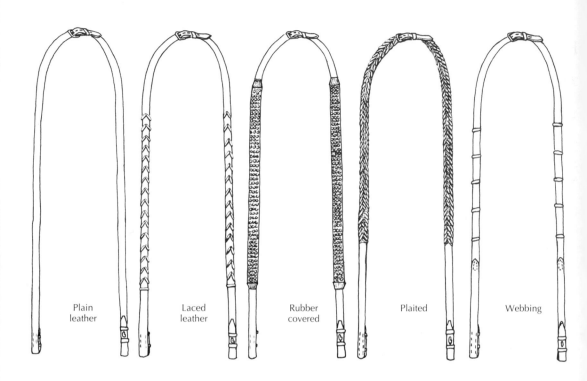

| Plain leather | Laced leather | Rubber covered | Plaited | Webbing |

Types of rein.

(10in) from the bit, they split into five strands which are then plaited right up to the buckle attachment. Although they provide a little more grip than plain leather ones, they also become slippery when wet.

Laced leather These are plain leather with a thin leather lace threaded through in a series of Vs, to form a hand-grip over the section of rein that is held.

German web These are the most popular non-leather reins. They, too, provide a good hand grip which is achieved by placing small leather slots, spaced approximately 10cm (4in) or 13cm (5in) apart, along the hand area.

Dartnall These are soft, plaited, cotton reins, shaped to the rider's hand. They are very light and kind on the hands, which helps the rider to maintain a sensitive contact.

Plaited nylon These are best avoided as they are slippery and easily slide through the hands.

FIXING

There are four main ways of securing reins to the bit:

1. The most common, and undoubtedly the best, is the hook-stud fastening.
2. They can be looped around the bit and sewn on.
3. Less common is the buckle fastening.
4. A simple loop fastening, where the long end of the rein is looped around the bit and then passed through a leather keeper that is sewn onto the back of the rein.

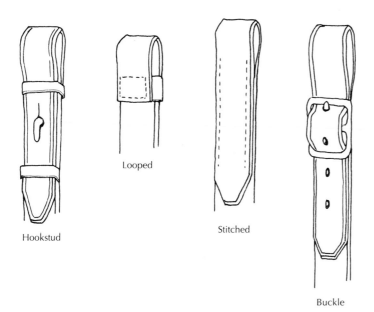

Hookstud

Looped

Stitched

Buckle

Ways of fixing the rein to the bit.

A bitless bridle can provide the solution to a variety of bitting problems. For example:

- A teething youngster.
- A horse with a sore mouth caused either by disease or injury. (However, if an injury has been caused by poor riding, it is the standard of the riding that needs to be improved rather than the bridle changed!)
- A horse who has some form of mouth abnormality, where bitting might prove painful.
- A horse who will not accept any kind of bit.

HOW A BITLESS BRIDLE WORKS

There are various types of bitless bridle and although they all work in much the same way, some are stronger than others. In simple terms, they control the horse by applying pressure to the nose, poll and curb groove. They can be very effective, although it can be harder to steer a horse in one, especially if he is not highly responsive to other aids.

TYPES OF BITLESS BRIDLE

Hackamore

Many people refer to all bitless bridles as hackamores, although this is incorrect. A hackamore is simply one type of bitless bridle. The jumping hackamore is the one seen in modern equestrian sports. It is quite mild as it has no lever action. It works instead by applying direct pressure to a rolled, padded noseband which is fixed to forked cheekpieces, to aid stability. The reins attach directly to rings on the noseband, which is open under the jaw, so any pressure on the reins simply puts pressure on to the horse's nose. A jowl strap secures the bridle under the jaw.

Blair's Pattern

This is the type people often think of when a hackamore is mentioned. However, it is quite different in that it operates on a leverage system, similar to a curb bit. There are two basic types: the English

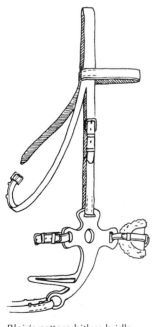
Blair's pattern bitless bridle.

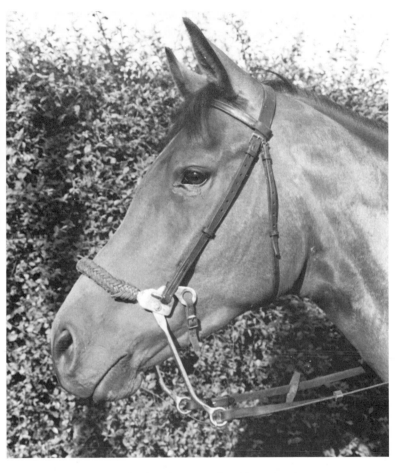

The German design often referred to as a German hackamore.

design, which has fairly short wide, flat cheekpieces, usually around 13cm (5in) in length; and the German design, which has a rolled noseband to concentrate the pressure, with much longer cheekpieces which can be seen up to about 30cm (12in). The longer the cheekpiece, the more the leverage, and thus the more severe the action.

Scawbrig

This is useful in that it can be used with or without a bit. In its simplest form, it comprises a noseband with rings, similar to a drop noseband, without the lower strap. Instead, a long strap, which makes the reins, is threaded through the rings and sits on the curb groove.

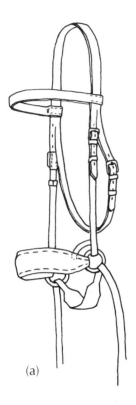

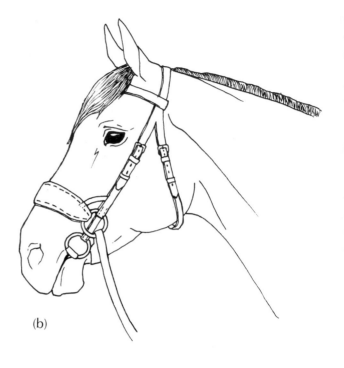

(b)

(a)

The Scawbrig: (a) without bit; (b) with bit but no reins. Reins can be attached to the bit when the horse is ready for the action of the bit to be introduced. The Scawbrig also sometimes incorporates a jowl strap.

If desired, a bit can be fitted on its own slip-head, without reins attached, to get the horse used to a bit in his mouth without any pressure being applied. In time, reins can be put onto the bit, and its action introduced gradually.

PROBLEMS

If the noseband of a bitless bridle is fitted too low it can cut off breathing and cause great distress.

It is easy to think you can do less harm with a bitless bridle, as there is no mouth to be rubbed and damaged. However, the horse's nose is almost as sensitive as his mouth, so a bitless bridle needs to be handled just as sensitively. Unfortunately, many novice riders pull too much in an attempt to control their horses, and the horse then pulls back even harder.

In many cases of difficulty with bitless bridles, it is simply not the horse at fault but the rider's inability to give precise seat, leg and voice aids; this is especially so if the rider has relied on a bit to do the steering and braking for them in the past.

The simplest piece of equipment used on the horse, and yet the most essential, is the headcollar. Without it we cannot catch him, lead him, tie him up or generally handle him safely.

Most headcollars are designed for everyday wear, although some are made for showing, either in white webbing or leather, which is often prettily stitched.

MATERIALS

Headcollars are most commonly made of leather or nylon. Leather is strong and easily cleaned but can be expensive as the leather is very thick and the stitching is usually done by hand. However, they are an excellent investment because, properly cared for, they will last a lifetime.

Nylon ones are also easily cleaned, but do not have as long a life span. With wear they can fray, but unless damaged in some way

A good-quality leather headcollar, which in this case was made to measure.

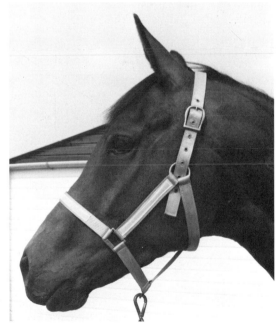

A nylon headcollar with reflective panels. Note how the lead-rope clip faces the horse's neck.

they are very unlikely to break under pressure in an emergency. This can be a problem if the horse has not been tied up correctly on to a piece of baling twine with a quick-release knot.

FITTING

Headcollars mainly come in pony, cob and full sizes, although many are adjustable and fit a range of horses. Some have only an adjustable noseband, while others also have an adjustable throat-lash. The noseband of a headcollar should lie about 5cm (2in) from the horse's cheekbones. It should fit snugly so that it cannot get caught on fence posts or bolts, but not so tightly that it restricts the horse from opening his mouth.

HALTERS

These are made of webbing or rope, and are usually an all-in-one design where the lead rope and halter are one long length. They are used extensively in studs and in training yards, because the one size can be adjusted to fit any horse. Once adjusted to fit, a knot should be tied at the point where the lead rope meets the halter in order to prevent the noseband from tightening should the horse pull back when tied up.

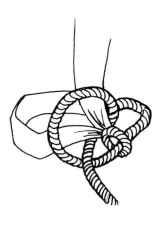

A webbing halter.

A foalslip.

HEADCOLLARS FOR FOALS

A headcollar designed for a foal is called a foalslip. It is always made of leather and is highly adjustable to allow for growth, which at such a young age takes place daily. Most foalslips have a 16cm (6in) length of leather attached to the ring on the noseband under the foal's jaw. This enables him to be held and lead without having to put on a lead rope each time.

LEAD ROPES

These are simple ropes with which to lead or tie up a horse. They can be made of cotton, which often comes in all sorts of colours, or heavy jute, or of nylon. Nylon lead ropes can fray and cause nasty burns if pulled violently through ungloved hands.

The clips that attach rope to headcollar are usually the snap hook variety. These are potentially dangerous if attached incorrectly. The point of the hook should always face the horse's neck.

A saddle is the most expensive single item of tack you will ever need to buy for your horse. It is obvious, then, that considerable time should be spent in choosing one as the wrong decision could prove disastrous. When buying a saddle it is necessary to consider the following:

- How much you can afford to spend. Less money does not necessarily mean a poorer-quality saddle. Some saddles bear a fashionable maker's name, and it often seems that this is what the buyer pays for: the saddle might well be excellent, but then so might others that cost much less. If money is tight then a good-quality secondhand saddle is preferable to an inferior new one.
- The horse's conformation and comfort. Any saddle should be fitted by an expert before purchase. It is also necessary to ride in it to ensure that it still fits with the rider's weight in the saddle. If the horse plays up out of character then there may be a problem.
- The rider's comfort. Saddles also need to be fitted to the rider. Everyone is an individual and some find certain designs and sizes more comfortable than others. Common sizes range between 35cm (13¾in) and 45.7cm (17⅞in), from pommel to cantle.

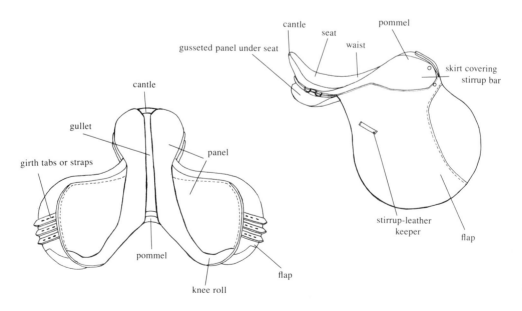

Parts of a saddle.

- Saddle condition. If secondhand, check that the tree is unbroken, that the padding is even, and that the leather is supple and strong. Always have an expert check the saddle before purchase.

THE SADDLE TREE

The tree is the skeleton of a saddle, around which the rest of the saddle is built. It can be rigid or sprung. As its name suggests, the rigid tree allows no movement. The spring tree allows a small amount of flexion which helps seat aids to be transmitted to the horse more effectively. The condition of a saddle's tree is all-important as a broken one can severely damage a horse's back.

If a broken tree is suspected, the saddle should not be used. To test the tree, hold the saddle upside down (seat facing the floor) between your legs. Grip the cantle and try to rock back and forth. If it does not give then it is sound. If it feels loose then it is likely to be broken. If in doubt always have it checked professionally.

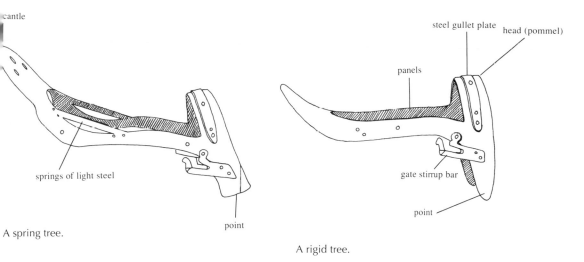

cantle

springs of light steel

A spring tree.

point

steel gullet plate

head (pommel)

panels

gate stirrup bar

point

A rigid tree.

CORRECT FITTING

The contribution that saddle fitting makes to performance is often neglected. When a horse misbehaves, we often suspect his teeth or his health, or perhaps his bit or even our own riding, but seldom do we suspect the saddle. However, if the saddle is not the correct size and width, or has not been correctly fitted, it will cause problems and the horse is then likely to try to let us know.

If your horse put his ears back or tried to nip you while you were tacking him up, or continually knocked fences down while jumping, or simply did not feel right while you were riding him, would you look to the saddle as a probable cause? Most likely you would not, saying, 'a well-fitting saddle is always a well-fitting saddle – isn't it?'

The answer is no. While it may have been an excellent fit initially, horses change and so do saddles. Horses change shape according to their work and condition, a fat horse can become slimmer and vice versa. A young horse can mature and change shape. The saddle flocking becomes flatter with wear. So ensuring correct fit is an ongoing responsibility.

Initial Fitting

This should be done by an expert; in the UK, by a member of the Master Saddlers Association. However, it is necessary for the rider also to know what to look for, so that potential problems can be spotted in the future.

Many saddlers will be happy to visit you with quite a few saddles, so that if your first choice is not suitable, you can select another.

Before selecting a saddle, the saddler will measure the horse's back and also assess his conformation, as poor conformation can dictate what type of saddle is most suitable. Most saddles come in narrow, medium or wide fittings.

When fitting, the saddler will ensure that:

To ensure a correct fit, check that you can place four fingers between pommel and wither.

Also check that you can see daylight through to the withers when viewed from behind.

- The tree of the saddle is the correct shape and width. If it is then he can finely adjust the way the saddle sits by inserting or removing the flocking as necessary. This is known as 'setting-up'.
- Once fitted, there is no pressure on or near the spine, with or without a rider; and that no weight is taken on the loins, but evenly spread over the lumbar muscles.
- The saddle sits even and level.
- The pommel does not put any pressure on the withers, either with or without a rider. Four fingers should be able to fit between the pommel and withers.
- Daylight can be seen through to the withers when viewed from behind.

- It does not restrict the horse's movement from the shoulder.

Fitting Problems

- Too much padding can cause a sore back as the saddle will have a tendency to rock from side to side causing friction points.
- Flat padding endangers the spine as the gullet can meet the back in extreme cases. Pressure points can also cause sores.
- A saddle that is too low at the pommel, or too wide, will rub the withers.
- If the padding is lumpy then localized pressure points will cause sores and discomfort.
- If the saddle looks as though it is perched on top of the back, with the pommel extremely high above the withers, then the tree is too narrow. The gullet of any saddle should be a minimum of 7.6cm (3in) wide all the way along.
- If the saddle swamps the horse, with the pommel very low at the wither, the tree is too wide.

DIFFERENT SADDLES FOR DIFFERENT DISCIPLINES

The General-Purpose Saddle

This is the saddle most used by the average rider for hacking, schooling and riding club activities. It is a compromise between a dressage and a jumping saddle. Most children's saddles are a scaled-down version of the general-purpose. A good choice is the Pony Club approved saddle.

The Dressage Saddle

The panel and saddle flap is straighter and longer than in the general-purpose saddle, to allow for the longer stirrup length needed for accuracy when performing complicated dressage movements. Knee and thigh rolls are placed so as to maintain a good leg position, allowing the rider to sit long and deep. Many dressage saddles have only two girth straps, which are longer than normal, for use with a Lonsdale girth (see page 52). This is to remove excess bulk from under the saddle flaps.

A general-purpose saddle with a
slant towards the dressage style.

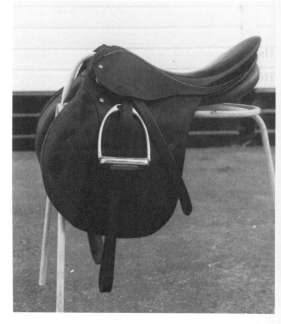

A general-purpose saddle with a
slant towards the jumping style.

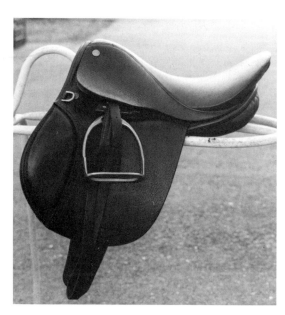

A scaled-down version of the general-
purpose saddle, for children.

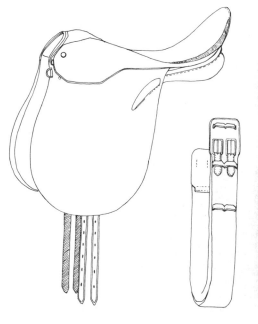

A dressage saddle with Lonsdale
girth.

The Showjumping Saddle

This saddle has a more rounded, forward-cut panel and flap. The knee rolls are also more pronounced so that the knee fits snugly when in the forward position. The seat can be very deep, or less so, depending on the rider's personal preference. While most riders can make do with a general-purpose saddle up to a jump height of 1.7m (3½ft), a purpose-made showjumping saddle is of great benefit thereafter.

The Long-Distance Saddle

This type of saddle is being developed constantly as the activity grows in popularity. Its main purpose is to spread the rider's weight over as large an area as possible to reduce the risk of creating localized pressure points. Specially designed numnahs are also used to reduce such risks. Since these saddles get a lot of use they need to provide maximum comfort for both horse and rider, and need to be extremely hard wearing.

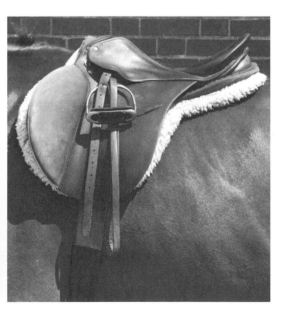

A showjumping saddle with forward-cut panel.

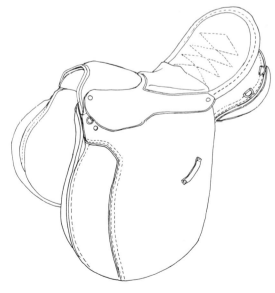

A long-distance saddle built with comfort in mind.

A side-saddle showing the two pommels.

The Side-Saddle

Most side-saddles are designed so that the rider's legs are on the near side of the horse. It should have a relatively flat seat, which is wide and level from side to side and from back to front. The seat is often covered in doeskin to prevent the rider from slipping. There are two pommels, which enable the rider to balance: one is fixed and the other (called the leaping head) is adjustable to suit the size of the rider's thigh.

The Show Saddle

This saddle is designed with a straight flap which slopes backwards to show off the horse's front and shoulder to its best advantage. Most have a rigid tree as these are flatter than the spring tree and so sit long and low so as not to detract too much from the horse's top line. However, they do not give very much thought to the rider and so may not feel as comfortable as the horse's normal saddle.

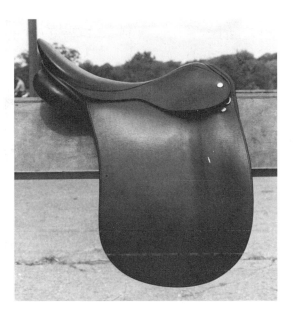

A show saddle.

Some show saddles have full panels.

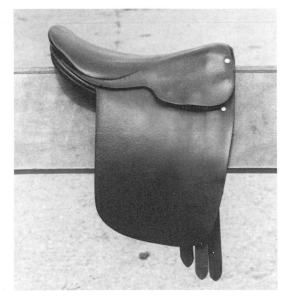

Others, like this pony show saddle . . .

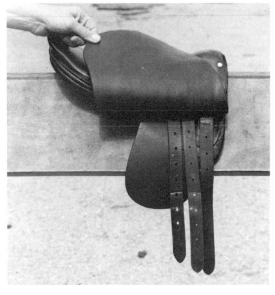

. . . have only a half panel to remove bulk from under the rider's leg.

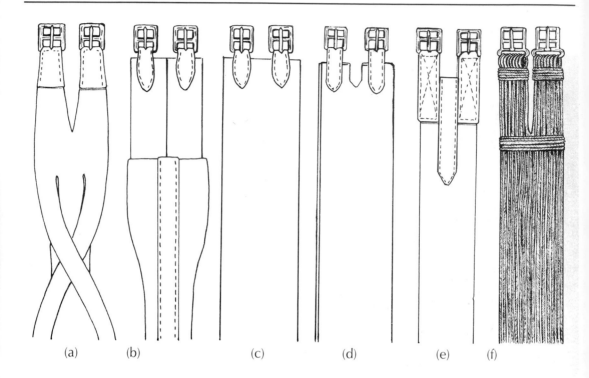

(a)   (b)   (c)   (d)   (e)   (f)

(a) Balding girth; (b) Atherstone; (c) Lampwick; (d) Three-fold; (e) Foam-padded (Cottage Craft); (f) German cordstring.

The girth keeps the saddle in place, and although it is a simple piece of equipment, there are nevertheless important considerations which need to be taken into account when selecting and using it.

GIRTH DESIGNS

Leather

The Balding pattern One of the most popular girths, its special design, where the leather splits into three and crosses over, helps to prevent chafing and girth galls as it is narrower behind the horse's elbow.

The Atherstone pattern This girth is also shaped behind the elbow, although it is a single length girth (not split). Most commonly seen in leather, it can also be made of other materials and can be fitted with an elastic insert, or preferably one on each side, to provide a little 'give'.

The three-fold girth This is usually made of baghide, with an oiled fabric insert to keep the leather supple. When fitted, the rolled edge should face forward to prevent the open edge pinching.

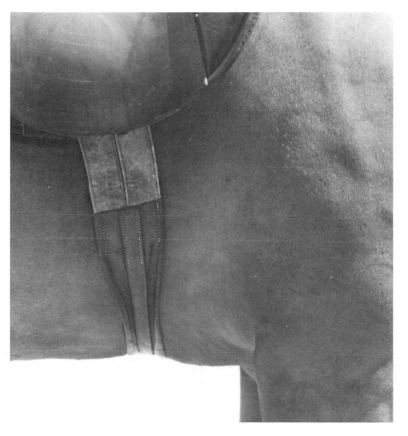

An Atherstone girth, clearly showing the curved section to prevent rubbing at the elbow.

Permeable or Absorbent Material

Lampwick These girths were at one time the most popular design. Made of tubular wick, they are very comfortable and are one of the least likely to cause chafing and sores.

Foam padded cotton These girths are usually associated with the name 'Cottage Craft' who are now the market leaders. They are very comfortable for the horse and extremely easy to keep clean.

German cordstring These girths are made of thick cotton cords which are kept in place by evenly spaced cross-weave panels. They are ideal for keeping the saddle in place, where other girths tend to move, as the individual strands grip the coat, thus preventing slipping.

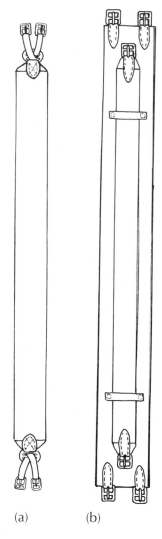

(a)   (b)

(a) Humane girth; (b)
Fitzwilliam.

Cheap nylon string   Not to be confused with the German cordstring, these are not recommended as they have caused pain to many horses.

Fitzwilliam and humane   These two girths are very logical patterns, but seem to have lost popularity. The Fitzwilliam often used to be seen on side-saddles but was also practical where extra security was needed as all three girth straps could hold the saddle in place.

The humane girth, which can be made from web or three-fold leather, employs a sliding strap through a ring, which allows a little 'give' similar in use to the elastic inserts.

Surcingle or Overgirth

An overgirth is used as an extra security measure when riding across country. It completely encircles the saddle and girth and is made of strong webbing, with an elastic insert to provide the 'give' during strenuous exercise. Choose one that has sufficient tabs to hold the end of the fastening strap securely in place, as an overgirth does up under the horse's tummy – a trailing strap could be irritating to the horse and potentially dangerous. A surcingle is another name for an overgirth, although surcingles are also used to secure rugs and are made in many different types of unpadded material.

Short Belly Girths

These are designed for use with dressage saddles, the best known being the Lonsdale design. They are intended to reduce bulk from under the rider's leg. Dressage saddles designed to take such girths have only two long girth straps. The belly girth which is consider-ably shorter than an ordinary girth, then does up to these straps below the saddle flap instead of under it. However, you should ensure that the buckles do up far enough away from the horse's elbow otherwise they can be uncomfortable and may cause sores.

LENGTH AND WIDTH

A girth should do up on equal holes either side of the saddle, usually mid-way up the girth strap. Most girths come in standard widths of between 9cm (3½in) and 11.5cm (4½in). Usually, for reasons of strength, the longer the girth the wider it is, unless it is an overgirth or a particular design such as the Lonsdale.

The importance of choosing suitable stirrups is often not appreciated, and many people settle for the ones that are on the saddle at the time of purchase.

COMMON DESIGNS

Basic pattern These are often referred to as English hunting irons. They are the most widely used, and are considered to be the best design for almost every purpose, except racing.

Peacock safety stirrups These have a thick, rolled rubber-band attached to the *outside* of the iron, so that in the event of a fall the rider's foot will easily be released from the stirrup as the band will simply pull off.

Kournakoff design These have an offset eye to the *inside*. The bars of the stirrup slope forward, and the tread should slope upwards to encourage the toe to sit higher than the heel.

Australian simplex or 'bent leg' These have a bulging forward bar on the *outside*. The idea is that in the event of a fall the foot cannot become trapped.

Bent top As their name implies, these have a 'bend' at the top. They should be fitted so that they slope forward, and are especially useful for those who have a tendency to push their foot well forward into the stirrup.

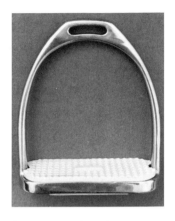

Basic pattern stirrup iron.

Peacock safety stirrup iron.

Australian simplex or 'bent leg' stirrup iron.

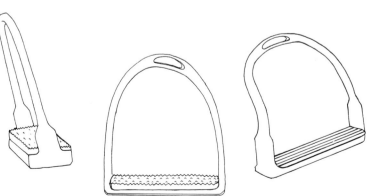

Kournakoff design. Bent top.

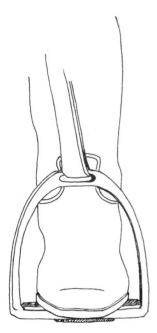

Irons should allow 1–1.5cm (⅜–⅝in) either side of your footwear.

TREADS

It is dangerous to ride in stirrup irons that do not have treads, as they provide a non-slip surface for the foot to rest upon. Treads are usually seen in black or white rubber, and have either straight ridges running across, or rows of raised pimples.

Most treads are flat for normal use, although ones that are built up on the outside are often seen in the dressage arena, enabling the rider to keep a very close contact with the inside of the leg.

SIZE AND WEIGHT

- Irons should be wide enough to allow 1–1.5cm (⅜–⅝in) either side of the rider's footwear.
- When measuring your boot for stirrups, take the measurement across the widest part of the sole as some soles protrude from the boot a good few millimetres either side, which will affect the width of iron required.
- Using an iron that is too small for you, may enable your foot to become jammed in it, which could lead to your being dragged in the event of a fall.
- Using too large a pair will enable your foot to slip forwards, right through the stirrup.
- Too light an iron will not stay put in the event of a fall, but will follow your foot, which could result in your being dragged.

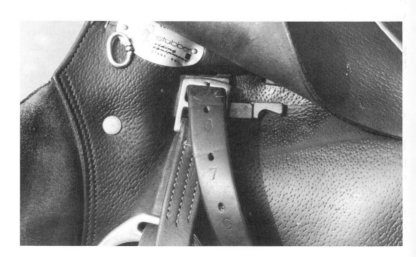

When riding, always make sure the stirrup-bar clip, is down.

Numnahs were originally designed to provide extra comfort for the horse when used under the saddle. In reality, it is because we as humans associate padding from pressure with comfort – and not particularly because the horse benefits from their use – that numnahs have become so popular. In fact, the reasons against the use of a numnah for almost all horses, far outweigh any arguments that might be put forward in their favour.

DISADVANTAGES

Firstly, a numnah *should* be unnecessary, as saddles are designed in all shapes and sizes and each is meant to be correctly fitted (with the aid of individual stuffing if necessary) to the horse who is to wear it. So the argument that a numnah should be used under the saddle to make it a better fit is not a valid one.

Secondly, a numnah can cause overheating of the back, which can make it tender and sore.

Thirdly, numnahs soon become soaked with sweat, which cools to leave a grimy layer of encrusted dirt on the side in contact with the skin. This causes irritation and chafing, leading to a sore back and, in some cases, skin disease.

It is therefore of paramount importance, if using a numnah, only to use a scrupulously clean one at all times. This can often be difficult with some numnahs because of the materials they consist of. A sheepskin numnah for instance, when it becomes wet, will regularly form into twists and knots, which are often the cause of saddle sores.

Lastly, a numnah defies the object of saddle design, as it puts greater bulk between rider and horse, when the aim is in fact to bring the two closer together.

ADVANTAGES

It is acceptable to use a thin saddle cloth as this helps to keep the panels clean, although, again, the cloth should be regularly cleaned.

Some horses seem to appreciate a numnah and go more freely as a result of its use, but they are often the exception to the rule, and may have some sort of underlying back trouble.

While every horse should only wear a saddle that is well-fitting, it

A simple 'straight' numnah, which is secured by tying the straps around the saddle panel.

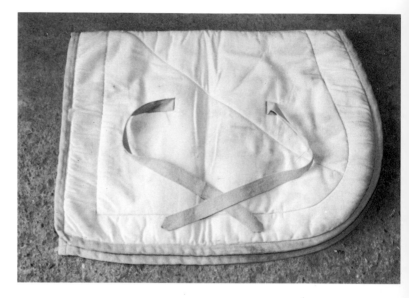

is a sad fact that all too often in riding and trekking centres horses have to share saddles. In such a situation it is preferable to use a numnah on each horse to prevent damage being caused by the ill-fitting saddle rubbing the skin and from pressure where novice riders bounce up and down at the wrong time. Needless to say, numnahs should be thick enough to afford such protection, and a clean one should be used for each horse.

DESIGN

Numnahs can be bought in the shape of different saddles. For example, it is possible to buy a dressage-shape numnah, a jumping shape, and so on, and they are usually available in three sizes: pony, cob or full size.

Some numnahs are made with a piece of padding or sheepskin sewn on to the wither area to offer extra protection should the numnah slip and lie flat over the withers. Others have long thin-shaped panels sewn in all the way along the back to offer extra cushioning where saddle and back meet, without adding extra bulk beneath the rider's leg.

Various methods are used to attach numnahs to the saddle, the most common being a sewn strap with looped ends on each side, through which one or all of the girth straps pass. In this case, the loops fit above the buckle guards to prevent them from slipping down. A strap through which the girth itself passes may also be sewn on to the bottom of the numnah flap.

Other methods of securing numnahs include:

- Straps that pass around the whole saddle panel and fasten with velcro.
- Strap and buckle arrangements.
- Straps that simply tie together.
- Pockets in the bottom of the numnah flap into which the saddle panel sits snugly, with the girth passing over the top or, in some cases, through a specially cut slit.

FITTING

The numnah should be large enough to protrude about 2–3cm

Care should be taken to ensure the numnah fits high into the saddle arch.

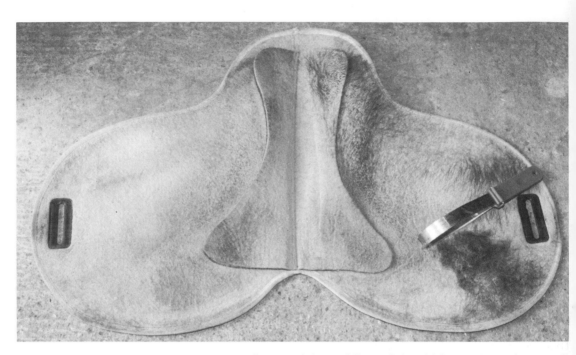

Removing hair from a numnah with a hair-scraper will prevent your washing machine from becoming clogged.

(¾–1¼in) all around the saddle and should fit snugly so that it will not slip back when in use. Care should be taken to ensure the numnah fits high into the saddle arch and does not stretch tightly over the withers as this will cause rubbing leading to wither sores: pull the numnah up into the saddle arch before tightening the girth. Care must also be taken to ensure the numnah lies completely flat under the saddle, without wrinkling.

MATERIALS

Numnahs are made in a variety of materials and colours, from the traditional sheepskin and felt, to the more modern synthetic materials.

While sheepskin numnahs are a good investment – properly cared for they will last for years – they are time consuming. Firstly they can only be washed by hand, and secondly the twists and knots that regularly form need to be laboriously combed out.

Most other synthetic materials are machine-washable, but some have leather straps which would prevent their being put into the machine.

Martingales can be considered 'extra' items of tack, although many people use them as standard. While the horse may have no need for one in the manège, excitement often takes over when jumping or hacking and so it may be safer to use one in these circumstances. Used and fitted correctly, they can ensure safety, and prevent unnecessary battles between you and your horse.

Fitted correctly, a martingale is passive and therefore does not act upon the horse unless he tries to evade his rider by throwing his head up, in which case it will help you to regain control as quickly as possible by preventing him from smashing you in the face!

The important thing to bear in mind when using one, is that it is not there to strap the horse's head down in any way.

The two most commonly used designs are the running martingale and the standing martingale.

THE RUNNING MARTINGALE

Fitting

The running martingale is a length of leather that runs from the girth and splits into two branches at the breast. Each branch has a ring through which the reins pass, anchored around the neck by a neckstrap.

Correct fitting is all important. The tighter the strap, which runs from girth to reins, the greater the restriction on the bit, so care must be taken to adjust the strap correctly. 'Textbook' fitting, is to have the rings in line with the withers when held up; however, this is often a little too loose to be of much use. About two holes shorter is more effective for most horses. Once fitted, the straps should be loose enough to allow the reins to come straight to the hand without any angle being created by the pull of the straps.

Rubber or leather rein-stops are a must. These are positioned between the bit and martingale rings to prevent the rings from running so far up the rein that they catch on the bit or rein fastenings.

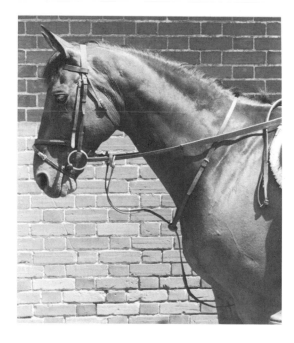

A running martingale. Note that it does not put any pressure on the reins while the horse's head is in the correct position.

Use

The running martingale has a more complex action than the standing variation. Because the reins pass through the rings, when the horse lifts his head beyond the adjusted limit, pressure is applied to the bit, exerting a downward force on the mouth. Through this action, the horse learns not to evade the bit by trying to throw his head in the air. The aim should be to use the martingale as a means to an end. Once the horse has learned not to throw his head up, and to work in a more pleasing outline, the martingale should be removed for further schooling.

THE STANDING MARTINGALE

Fitting

The standing martingale has a single length of leather which runs from girth to noseband, and which is also anchored by a neckstrap. It is correctly fitted when it can be pushed up the line of the gullet until it reaches about 10cm (4in) from the throat.

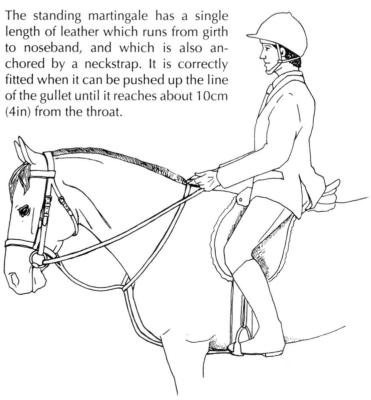

Standing martingale.

Use

The standing martingale was once very popular and although it is still used today, it is seen less frequently. This is not to say that it does not have its uses.

Downward pressure is exerted on to the nose through the noseband. The design is more restrictive than the running martingale, as the rider cannot allow the horse to have a free head should he so desire. Once the horse has thrown his head up to a point where he reaches contact with the martingale he is simply pulling against the girth.

Apart from polo ponies, who wear them as standard, the standing martingale is most useful for horses who have developed a bad habit of violently throwing their heads up, often without warning, which can result in the horse smashing his rider in the nose with his poll.

Bib martingale.

Fitted correctly the standing martingale does not inhibit a horse while jumping.

VARIATIONS

The bib martingale The action of this martingale is exactly the same as the running martingale. The only difference between the two is that the bib has a leather centrepiece between the straps to prevent excited horses from getting caught up. It can be useful for very excitable youngsters, or for the horse who continually tries to grab at the martingale straps.

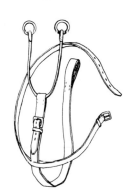

The pulley martingale.

The pulley This is another variation on the running martingale, where, instead of the strap dividing into two, it comes to a loop through which a cord with a ring at each end runs. The reins then pass through these rings as with the running design. Its advantage is that the horse can bend his head sideways without being restricted from the opposing rein.

The combined martingale This design was used quite often on many showjumpers until a few years ago. As its name suggests, it combines both a single strap attached to the noseband and dividing straps attached to the reins with rings. Thus, its action is that of both the running and standing martingale with pressure being applied both on the nose and on the mouth.

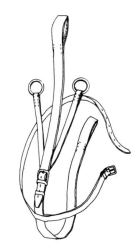

The combined martingale.

An Irish martingale.

The Irish martingale This design has no effect upon head carriage. It is simply a device to hold the reins together under the horse's neck and prevent them from being thrown over the horse's head should the rider fall.

The Market Harborough Some people would put this design in the training aids section, but, in common with other martingales, it only comes in to play when the horse raises his head above an accepted height, so its rightful place is in the martingale group.

The rider has much more control, however, and so one needs to be experienced in its use before fitting and using it. When used

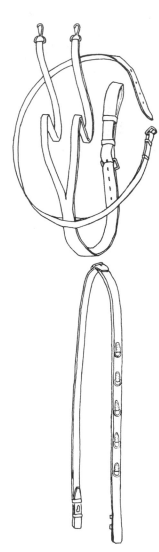

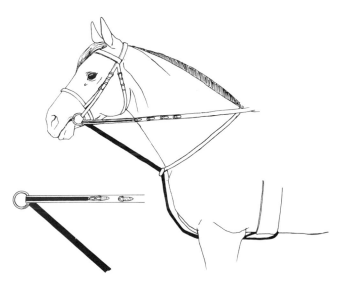

correctly, the effect on the horse is similar to that of a running martingale, but instead of the two dividing straps ending in rings, they are much longer and end in snap-hooks, which run through the bit and attach to immovable D-rings on the reins. There are usually four Ds to each rein, so the martingale can be adjusted longer or shorter, to be more or less severe depending on how far up the rein you clip the snap-hooks.

PROBLEMS

The biggest problem with martingales is that people often have

The Market Harborough.

them adjusted too tightly. This is especially true when jumping. It would seem they are used in this way in the hope of gaining more control, when in fact, because the horse is being unnaturally restrained, he will often fight harder to try to relieve the extreme downward pressure being exerted. Too tight a martingale can also be counter-productive as the horse learns to lean on it, helping himself to balance and thus developing an incorrect outline.

BREASTPLATES

Many breastplates have a ring at the breast, to which separate martingale attachments can be fixed. A breastplate is used to prevent the saddle from slipping backwards, and is especially useful when jumping. It attaches to the saddle by means of two adjustable leather straps which go through two rings on the breastplate and fix to the Ds on either side of the front of the saddle.

Horses whose conformation encourages the saddle to slip backwards should always wear a breastplate.

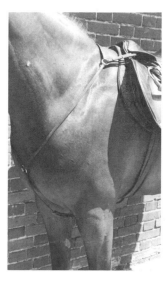

A breastplate.

BREASTGIRTHS

The Aintree breastgirth   This fastens around the chest, but does not have a girth loop. Instead, two loops fit around the girth on either side of the saddle. This design is more usually seen on horses competing cross-country or racing, and is a safety measure to prevent the saddle slipping backwards, especially where lightweight saddles are used. Care must be taken when fitting, to ensure it will not interfere with the horse's wind pipe. Correctly fitted it should lie just above the point of the horse's shoulder.

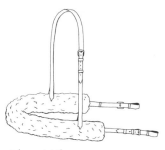

A breastgirth.

NECKSTRAPS

These are simple straps of leather placed around the neck to offer riders something to grip on to if they lose balance. Many riding schools simply use a stirrup leather, but this can ride up and slip around the horse's neck.

The best neckstraps are those that consist of a handle attached to the top of a breastplate with correct attachments to the saddle and girth, as they provide more security when needed.

Training aids are often referred to as 'gadgets', as though they in some way devalue the skills of the rider or trainer. This is not very helpful to the average rider, who through such prejudice often perseveres with a problem without resorting to a training aid, when using one might enable him to solve a certain problem and move on to a better relationship with his horse.

The best definition of a gadget in equestrian terms is 'a useful piece of equipment employed to make a task easier'. The task is usually to encourage the horse to work in a nice round outline. The gadget will help to round the front end while the rider produces the power from the back end – engaging the hocks – through correct riding. A gadget is not, however, a short cut for those who have neither the patience nor the ability to train their horses properly.

The use of gadgets will always be controversial and only the individual can decide whether to use them or not. If you do use a gadget you should be meticulous with its fitting and use. Used carelessly they can actually do a lot of damage, so they should be used only under supervision until you are experienced enough to know what you want to achieve and to recognize the 'feel' of the desired effect.

Guidelines for correct use of training aids:

- Ensure correct fit and adjustment.
- Use them only with a snaffle bridle.
- Introduce them slowly and increase their action gradually.
- Do not use in-hand training aids for ridden work and vice versa, unless designed to do so.
- Set a goal and work towards it methodically.
- Once the aim is accomplished, cease to use the aid.

AIMS

When selecting a training aid, think hard about what you are trying to achieve.

- Do you want to encourage the horse to work in a more pleasing outline? If so, is your own riding up to scratch? It is harmful to use an aid to encourage a correct outline if you do not know what a correct outline is.
- Do you want to cure a bad habit? If so, can you be sure that it is not your own riding that is causing the problem? A bad habit is often only a symptom, so first you must identify the cause.

RIDDEN AIDS

Draw Reins

These are the most commonly used training aid. They run from the girth, up between the horse's forelegs, then through the bit rings to the rider's hands. They should always be used with an ordinary pair of reins so they are only brought into play when necessary and can be relaxed when the horse complies with your instruction. When used correctly, they encourage the horse to drop his nose and lower his head.

Draw reins.   Running reins.

Running Reins

These run from the girth, either side of the saddle, and through the bit rings to the rider's hands. These also need to be used with ordinary reins. Their effect is to take up the strain when a horse pulls or leans on the bit, encouraging him to drop his nose.

Pulley System

The Abbot-Davies balancing rein and the de Gogue can, in expert hands, produce extraordinary results where other schooling

The de Gogue fitted correctly for ridden work.

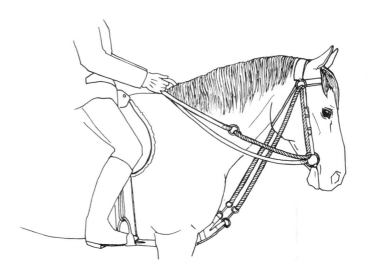

methods have failed. However, their action is extremely precise and can be powerful, so they are best left to the experts.

IN-HAND AIDS

Side-Reins

These are the most commonly used accessory when lungeing, and are used almost universally on youngsters to introduce rein contact. They fix on to the girth strap under the saddle flap at one end, and then on to either the lungeing cavesson or bit rings at the other end, depending on the stage of training. They should be fitted fairly loosely, so that the horse can make contact with them. If they are fitted too tightly, in an attempt to gain the correct head carriage, they will simply cause the horse discomfort which he will object to by trying to evade them.

They are mostly made of plain leather although some have elastic or rubber-ring inserts to provide a little give.

The Chambon

The Chambon is useful for a horse who evades the side-reins by coming behind the bit. Instead of running directly from saddle to the bit, the reins pass through two metal rings attached to a specially

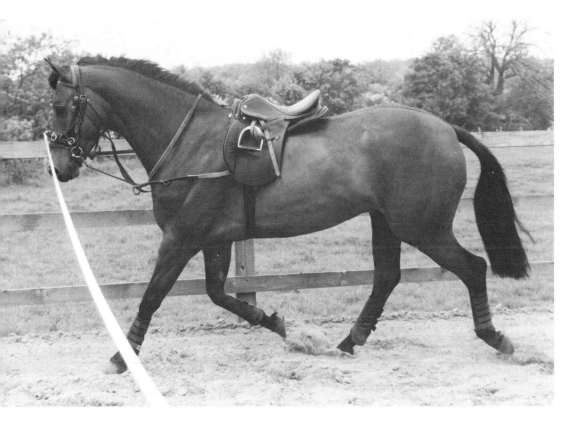

Side-reins are the most common lungeing accessory.

The Chambon.

The de Gogue fitted correctly for lungeing.

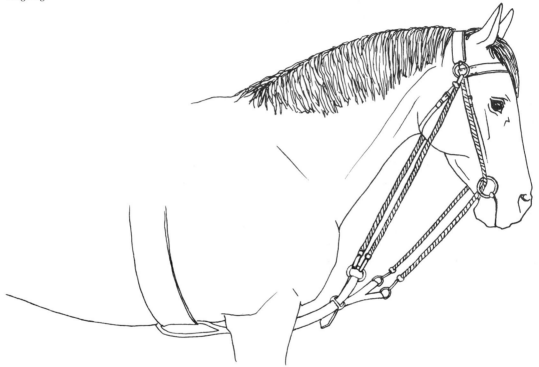

designed headpiece. They work with the horse, rather than providing a dead contact. Should he raise his head, pressure is applied to the mouth and poll, encouraging him to lower it again. When he complies the pressure is released. They produce very good results when trying to achieve a nice long and low outline with a youngster. The horse that works well in the Chambon may well appreciate the action of the de Gogue when ridden, rather than other training aids.

The Equi Train

This is a weight which simply clips on to the bit to encourage the horse to lower his head without being able to lean on any rein. The Equi train comes in three different weights which apply more or less poll pressure as desired.

An Equi Train.

There are two main uses for boots and bandages: one is to provide protection when travelling; the other is to provide protection and support when schooling or competing. Bandages are also used for veterinary purposes.

TRAVELLING

Bandages

Travelling bandages are not used very much anymore as they are time-consuming to put on. However, if they are to be used there should be sufficient padding under them to provide plenty of protection. Gamgee is the best padding for the job, and the piece used needs to be long enough to extend from the coronet to well above the knee. The gamgee should be folded around the leg with the end facing towards the back. The bandage, which starts below the knee, should also be wound around the leg in the same direction. They are usually made of a woollen type of material.

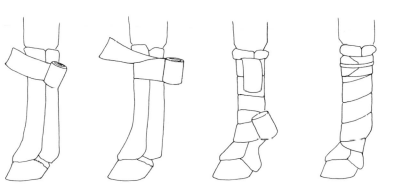

How to bandage for travelling.

Boots

Being taken in a vehicle is a very unnatural thing for horses and they often feel insecure. Some horses will plant their feet and refuse to move until the vehicle stops. Others will constantly move their feet in an attempt to gain security. As a result they often bang their legs on the partitions or knock one leg with the other. Horses also knock their hocks against the back wall and some even go down on their knees. It is our job to protect the horse against potential injuries and the simplest way of doing so is to fit travelling boots.

A horse with protective clothing for travelling.

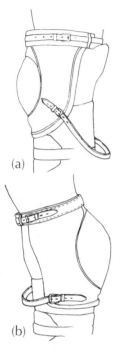

(a) Knee boots for use when travelling; (b) hock boots for use when travelling.

A type of poll guard.

At one time, travelling boots only protected from under the knee, or hock, down to the coronet. Nowadays, travelling boots are all-in-one and extend from the coronet right over the knee. They are usually made of well-padded, synthetic materials that are light, prevent sweating and are easily cleaned. Most fasten with velcro straps.

If the shorter type of travelling pads are used, then knee and hock boots are also needed for protection. They have blocked and stuffed leather knee and hock caps, providing good protection from knocks to the joints. They have two straps to secure the boot. The top strap is done up tightly enough so that the boot will not slip down over the joint, and an elastic insert allows a little give. The lower strap is fairly long and is done up loosely to allow the horse to bend his joint without restriction. Unlike other boots, the straps always do up facing forward.

Other Travelling Equipment
- Tail guard or bandage to prevent rubbing.
- Poll guard (made of felt or leather) to prevent injury if the horse hits his poll on the roof.
- A rug or sheet (depending on the time of year) to prevent the horse from rubbing his sides against the partitions and to keep him warm from draughts.

RIDDEN WORK

Bandages

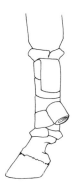

How to bandage for exercising.

Bandages used for ridden work are called exercise bandages. They are slightly elasticated and are about 7cm (2¾in) wide. They, too, should have gamgee underneath, although this only needs to cover from the fetlock joint up to the knee. They are applied in the same direction as a travelling bandage, although it is important to achieve an even pressure all the way down the leg.

Boots

Brushing boots   These are the most frequently used boots. They prevent the horse's fetlock joints from being rubbed and bruised when they brush against each other while the horse is being lunged or ridden. They can have straps and buckles or velcro fastenings.

Tendon boots   These come in various types but they are all designed to offer support for the tendons when doing strenuous work. Open-fronted tendon boots are used on the forelegs to protect the tendons from being struck with the hind feet. This is called a high overreach. Some designs also act as brushing boots.

Overreach boots   These are bell-shaped boots which protect the coronet and bulbs of the heel. They fit around the pastern and completely cover the hoof. They are made of rubber. Some have buckle or velcro fastenings, while others simply pull over the hoof.

A brushing boot.

A tendon boot.

An overreach boot.

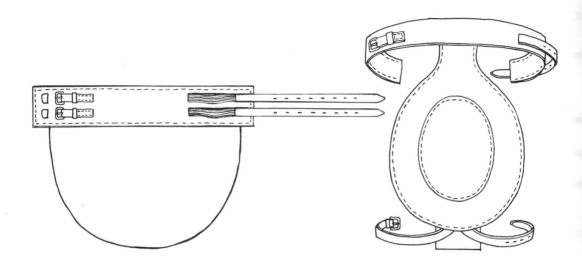

Skeleton knee pads.

A sausage boot.

Skeleton knee pads   These are a lighter type of knee boot designed for riding on the roads. They offer protection against broken knees in the event of a fall.

Sausage Boots

These are not used for exercise or travel, but are intended to prevent the horse from bruising his elbow with his shoe while lying in the stable or field. They are a ring made of rubber or padded leather and look a little like a doughnut, which fits around the pastern when needed.

FITTING BOOTS

No boot should be put on a horse unless his legs are perfectly clean. As with other forms of tack, boots fitted on top of dirt and dried sweat will rub the horse causing sore patches. Boots are designed only for short-term use, so they should not be used when out hunting for the day, as dirt will work its way inside the boots and cause chafing.

Guidelines for the fitting and use of boots:

- Make sure the right boots are put on the right legs. Boots come in pairs, although there may be four to a set. Front boots are often shorter than hind boots, and they usually have one strap less.
- The straps do up facing the rear, with the exception of knee and hock boots (*see* page 70).
- The straps do up on the outside of the leg to prevent their being rubbed open by the opposite leg.
- When fitting, do up the middle strap first. This will prevent the boot from sliding down the leg should the horse decide to move off before the boot is fully secure.
- Fasten the boots tightly enough so that they do not slip but not so tightly that they are uncomfortable. As with bandages, the pressure should be even all the way around the leg.
- If the boots are fastened with leather straps, use the keepers to prevent them from coming undone.
- When unfastening boots, work from the bottom upwards.
- It is extremely important that velcro fastenings are kept free of dirt. Dirty velcro is less effective and so straps start to come undone, which could cause an accident if out riding, or if lungeing.

Preventing Injuries

Some of the injuries that can be prevented by wearing protective boots include:

- Interference injuries: knocks, bruises and cuts caused by one leg or hoof 'interfering' with another.
- Broken knees: injuries to the surface of the knee, which can be minor, or very severe where the knee bone is exposed. They are most often caused by stumbling and falling on a hard road surface, without the protection of knee boots.
- Knocks caused by hitting show jumps or cross-country fences.
- Travelling injuries.

The general-purpose saddle is often used for all disciplines, but there are occasions when a specially designed saddle is needed, either for added security and effectiveness, or to show off the horse to his best advantage.

Various disciplines also often require the use of different bridles and accessories, whereas others frown upon the use of anything other than a simple snaffle or double.

DRESSAGE

In all but the most novice events, a specially designed dressage saddle will be needed, which may be black, brown, navy or grey, and of English or Continental style.

In Prelim and Novice events, a plain snaffle bridle (which must have a noseband fitted) is compulsory. However, the noseband may be a cavesson, flash or drop. (Grakle nosebands are allowed only for horse trials tests.) Elementary and Advanced Medium standards permit either an ordinary snaffle or double. For Advanced tests a simple double is used. Consult the relevant national rule book for permitted bits, as more are now allowed than were a few years ago.

Tack should be plain, but of high quality with a deep sheen to it, which adds to the elegance of the whole turnout.

SHOWJUMPING

An all-purpose saddle is often used for showjumping, but as the fences get larger, the need for more security increases the need for a specially designed jumping saddle.

Almost any bridle and accompanying accessories are used while showjumping, including the use of a whole range of different bits.

However, while very few items of tack are not allowed, certain correct combinations should be respected. For instance, a Market Harborough should only be used with a plain snaffle. Draw, running, and balancing reins are not allowed, and pony classes do not permit the use of Market Harboroughs or bitless bridles.

EVENTING

It is only in recent years that a cross-country or 'eventing type' of saddle has evolved. More emphasis is placed on the weight of the saddle itself as riders in advanced competitions need to keep within the bounds of an optimum weight. Many eventing saddles are similar in design to a general-purpose, and so many competitors simply use their ordinary saddle.

The bridle used will be whatever suits the horse best for each discipline, although as a guideline you should follow those discussed for the dressage phase and similarly for the showjumping phase.

Almost any tack is acceptable for showjumping.

Side-saddle is becoming more and more popular. As with many other showing classes, a double bridle is most usually used.

SHOWING

In all but the most minor competitions a showing saddle should be used.

While a double bridle is the most preferred for showing, snaffles and Pelhams are also permitted for many classes.

Side-Saddle

The recent revival in side-saddle riding has enabled side-saddle classes to be staged at many shows both nationally and locally, and ladies' hunters and hacks can also be ridden side-saddle.

As with other showing classes, a double bridle is most usually used.

LONG DISTANCE

Long-distance riding is one of the growth areas of the 1990s. Almost any tack can be used and synthetic tack seems to be very popular for this discipline.

The correct care of tack is extremely important for the comfort and safety of both horse and rider. Unfortunately, we have all seen even the top riders on television fall off because an article of tack has given way, so accidents *can* and *do* happen. Yet this is often a situation where people think 'It'll never happen to me!' Vigilance when cleaning, and regular maintenance, will reduce the risk.

CLEANING

After each ride, tack should be given a quick clean, then once a week it should be cleaned thoroughly.

The tack cleaning kit should consist of a clean bucket filled with tepid water, two sponges, a clean cloth, a duster, a small soft brush, a nail brush, a dandy brush, saddle soap, leather dressing, metal polish, a flat blunt knife, and a paper clip.

Leather

This is the most traditional material and is still as popular as ever. It is easy to clean and is comfortable for the horse. However, unless it is kept soft with glycerine saddle soap it will dry out and crack.

To clean tack thoroughly it is best to take it completely apart, so that all hidden areas can be seen to, and any faults spotted, although this is not necessary for each daily clean. The saddle should have the numnah, stirrups, leathers, girth and buckle protectors removed and the bridle should be stripped.

To clean tack properly, the procedure must be methodical and thorough:

1. Undo all buckles and either hang each piece of the bridle on a tack hook, or lay it flat on a clean surface. Put the saddle on to the saddle-horse. Put the bit, irons and treads, into the bucket of water to soak.
2. First use the soft brush on the dry leather to remove any particles of mud, as the grains of grit present in mud will scratch the leather if pulled along with a sponge.
3. The leather should then be washed. For straight items, hook one end on to the tack hook and hold taut with one hand. Wrap a damp sponge around each item and rub firmly up and down. Rinse the sponge regularly.
4. Remove hard lumps of grease, which collect on the underside of tack, with a flat, blunt knife, or a ball of horse hair.

When soaping, always wet the soap, not the sponge.

5. Allow the leather to dry under normal, airy conditions. Do not put it in the airing cupboard or by a radiator as this will dry out the natural oils.

6. Each item should then be soaped, preferably with a soap containing glycerine. This conditions the leather each time it is cleaned and so eradicates the need to apply oil or special dressings intended to keep the leather supple. As long as your tack is cleaned regularly in this way, suppling agents will be needed only if the leather gets drenched, when caught in pouring rain or falling in a water jump, for example.

7. When soaping, always wet the saddle soap and not the sponge. If too much water is used the soap will lather up and is more difficult to apply and less effective. Hold each piece as before and rub up and down on straight items and in circular movements on larger areas. Work the soap in until the leather becomes pliable in your hands and a rich sheen is achieved.

8. Pay particular attention to the underside of the leather (the area that comes into contact with the horse) as this is more absorbent and will give an indication of how dry the tack is. The curves in tack, such as where the stirrup leathers or bridle fastenings bend, should also be kept very supple. At every cleaning session, check for signs of weakness.

9. After soaping, use your paper clip to push out any saddle soap that has collected in buckle holes.

10. Wash the bit in clean water to remove any stale saliva and dried matter, and also wash the irons and treads. The treads should be brushed with the nail brush until all dirt is removed. White treads may need to be scrubbed with an ordinary household cleaner. These should then be dried and pushed back into the irons.

11. Occasionally, metal items such as buckles and saddle studs should be cleaned with metal polish, but *not* the bit.

12. Reassemble the tack to save time before a ride.

Cleaning Leather Accessories

Cleaning of tack does not stop with the saddle and bridle: such things as boots, rollers and rug straps also need to be cleaned although they are often overlooked. These should be treated in the same way as the bridle and the saddle for general cleaning. The leather straps on outdoor rugs often become caked in mud and get soaked in heavy rain. As a result these will need to be washed off and oiled regularly if they are to last. Protective boots also get very muddy and wet when hacking, so these should be treated similarly.

Exceptions to the Rule

The saddle seat, which is often made of softer leather, usually stays relatively clean, so will not need cleaning every time. However, when you do clean it you should ensure the saddle soap you are using does not stain, otherwise your jodhpurs will need to be treated with a stain remover!

If the seat of your saddle is made from a very soft leather it may have an aniline, dyed finish. This cannot be treated in the same way as ordinary leather, but should have a cream or wax-based product applied in line with the manufacturer's instructions.

The effect of using water and glycerine soap on tack finished in this way, is that patches will start to lose colour, turning your smart saddle into a leopard skin. If in doubt, seek advice from your saddler before cleaning.

Constant oiling of tack is unnecessary for articles that are regularly cleaned with glycerine soap. However, new tack needs to be oiled before use and a few more applications will be needed before it becomes supple. Special leather treatments are now available, or you can use pure neat's-foot oil, which will not rot the stitching. If tack is oiled too much it will become limp, and will wrinkle and seep oil when bent.

Other Materials

Metal   Stainless steel is by far the safest metal used in the production of stirrup irons, bits and buckles. The items needing the most care are buckles, as these consist of more than one piece and take a lot of pressure. To prevent corrosion of the metal, and in particular the tongue of a buckle, you should apply a layer of grease once a week. This will also need to be done on movable bit-ring joints.

Having washed any metal parts, you should dry them thoroughly with a cloth, as drip drying encourages corrosion.

Synthetic tack   Items manufactured from synthetic materials are very easy to maintain. Bridles are simply washed and saddles can even be hosed down. All synthetic tack can be disinfected, which is very valuable if a horse using it has contracted a contagious skin infection.

Synthetic tack makes light work
of tack cleaning: saddles can
simply be hosed down.

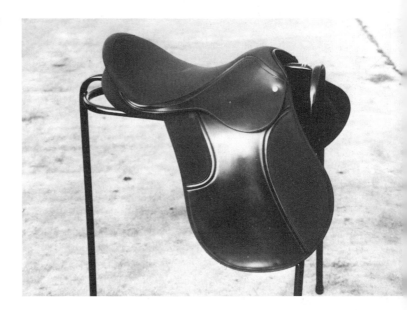

Fabrics Other fabrics used in the manufacture of tack range from
cotton to pure wool. Each item will firstly need to have the dirt and
horse's hair removed by brushing. It will then need to be washed,
either by hand or in the washing machine, depending on the material. If scrubbing by hand is necessary, you should use only a mild
soap or non-biological product, as rinsing is difficult and any cleaning agents remaining in the material can cause irritation.

Machine-washable items with buckles should be placed in a pillow case before they are put into a machine.

PUTTING-UP

To keep a bridle in good shape it should be hung on a semicircular
bracket. Reins can either be placed over the bracket as well, or
passed through the throat-lash and assembled in a figure-of-eight
design.

To ensure the saddle does not get damaged it should be put on to
a saddle rack and covered with a saddle cover or sheet. All other
straight lengths of leather should be hung by the buckles on hooks,
well above floor level. Other accessories, such as boots and rugs,
can be placed flat on a shelf or in a drawer, or hung up to air if at all
damp.

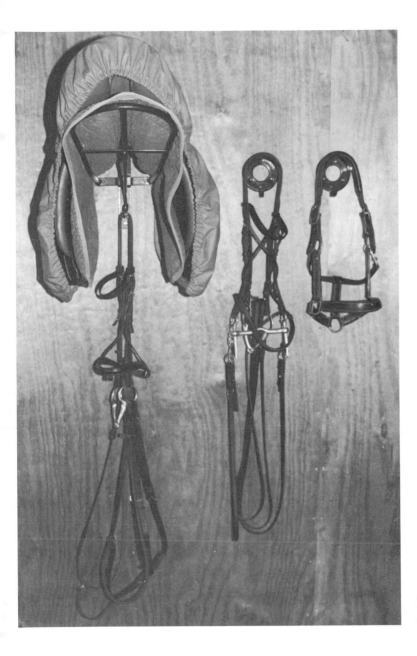

After cleaning always 'put up' your tack to keep it in good shape.

LONG-TERM STORAGE

If tack is not to be used for some time it should be packed and stored in a secure trunk. Leather items should be separated and each should have a thin layer of preservative applied, including the buckles. The items should then be wrapped in a cotton sheet and stored at room temperature, away from damp, insects or mice.

Saddles should be treated in the same way, and put on racks in a permeable cover. Polythene should not be used to cover leather as it encourages condensation which can lead to mildew.

Other materials should be cleaned and stored flat in a dry atmosphere, either in a trunk or a chest of drawers, with moth balls. Any repairs should be seen to before storing, otherwise they will be forgotten and will cause delay when the items are needed again.

RENOVATION AND SERVICING

If you notice minor defects in your tack while cleaning, you should have them seen to before you use the tack again. In any case you should endeavour to have your tack checked annually by your saddler who will attend to any areas of weakness.

Common Areas of Weakness

Stitching   Most problems occur when the stitching works loose or starts to rot. Items can be restitched by your saddler, at little cost, making them perfectly safe to use. Pay particular attention to items that take a lot of stress, such as stirrup leathers, girths and reins.

Saddle stuffing   This may become lumpy and uneven; in any case, it will gradually get flatter. At the first sign of deterioration the saddle should be restuffed by your saddler and refitted correctly to your horse.

Saddle tree   After a fall, or if the horse has rolled while wearing his saddle, the tree should be checked to make sure it has not broken. If you are in any doubt you should have your saddler check it.

The bit   The bit rings or joints can become loose with wear and should be checked regularly for signs of roughness. A bit cannot, or at least should not, be repaired; always replace it.

THE EFFECTS OF NEGLECT

Poorly maintained equipment will not last. Leather that is not

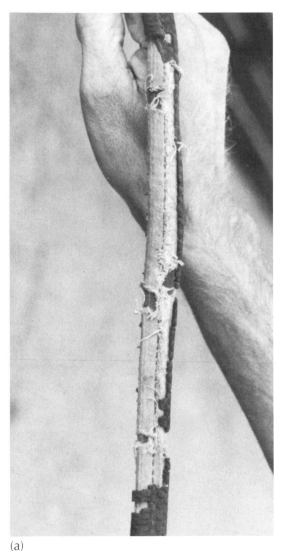

(a)

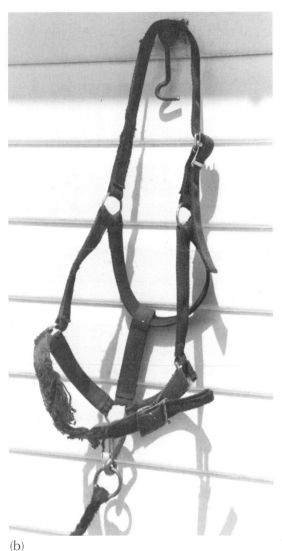

(b)

looked after will dry out and crack or even snap altogether; the stitching will rot; metal buckles can wear or become loose; non-leather materials will rot, wear, fray and tear, all of which can lead to more expense, safety risk, and injury to the horse from chafing or sharp articles. As the horse can only communicate his discomfort through his actions, he may well start to play up. Being thrown off because the horse is trying to rid himself of such discomfort, should not be the first we know of tack faults caused by poor maintenance.

Poorly maintained tack is a safety risk. These reins (a) could snap while you are out riding; and this headcollar (b) could result in a loose horse.

The reasons for using tack that fits the horse properly and for ensuring such tack is put on correctly are threefold: to ensure safety; to prevent injuries; and to ensure it actually does the job it is intended to do. So the consequences of badly fitting tack can be very serious.

SADDLE AND GIRTH SORES

A sore that develops as a result of the saddle or girth rubbing is often referred to as a gall. This is a thickening of the skin, which is a result of uneven pressure from the saddle, or a poorly fitting saddle that constantly rubs the horse. The most common sites for such galls are the withers and the middle of the back along the spine; although less common, they also appear either side of the back where the saddle panels cause constant friction points.

In all cases, the solution is to correct the saddle by restuffing or if possible by mending, or to replace the saddle altogether. In any case it is sensible to have a qualified person advise on the saddle and its fit before reusing it.

Using a thick numnah is not acceptable, even as a temporary measure, as it does not solve the problem, it merely masks it. However, sometimes sores do occur for reasons other than a badly fitting saddle: when a flabby horse comes up from grass, for example. In such cases a thick foam pad, with the area above the sore removed, can be used under a correctly fitting saddle until the sore has healed.

The girth area is another place that regularly develops sores. These sores, known as 'girth galls', can develop as a result of a soft, flabby horse wearing a tough leather girth; or because the girth constantly rubs back and forth while in use; or because the girth is too wide to sit comfortably in the centre of the horse's sternum curve. In the first two cases, the girth should be changed for a softer type, and the girth that is too wide should be changed for a narrower one.

Always ensure that the pressure from the girth is even. The girth should fix to at least the second hole on either side of the girth straps, and there should also be two spare holes above the buckles each side. So the important considerations are that the girth is the correct length, width and is secured evenly.

Rubber bit rings can be useful for a horse who objects to the pressure of the bit rings. They simply pull over the bit rings and protect the corners of the horse's mouth.

SORE MOUTHS

A bit that is not the correct width for the horse has the potential to cause soreness in the mouth. When a jointed snaffle is pulled straight, it should protrude about 5mm (¼in) either side of the horse's mouth.

As the corners of a horse's mouth are very sensitive, make sure there are no rough edges to the bit or bit rings and that any bit cheekpieces are not rubbing. If the horse seems to object to the pressure of the rings you can try using rubber bit stops.

Your horse's teeth may also cause problems if they are sharp, as the bit may come into contact with the cheek teeth causing sore cheeks.

A bit that is too strong can also cause a sore mouth. If a horse becomes too strong, people tend to use a more severe bit, which is often a mistake in the first instance because the horse may have become stronger because he finds the bit currently being used too severe for him. The only way he can inform us of this is to fight the bit every time it is used. If we then use an even stronger bit, the horse pulls even more.

All this pulling results in sores which could have been avoided by using a milder bit in the first place. So, knowing what *not* to use is as important as knowing what to use.

A soft girth sleeve.

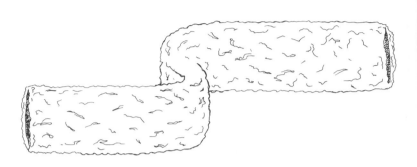

Applying surgical spirit to a girth gall.

PREVENTING SORES

Most sores can be prevented by only using tack which fits the horse properly and by ensuring it is put on correctly. Galls can further be prevented by making sure the horse is always clean underneath his tack, and by ensuring that the tack itself, including numnahs and girths, are always clean.

For horses known to have very sensitive skin, it is a good idea to use a soft girth sleeve over the girth, and possibly a soft, scrupulously clean numnah under the saddle.

To harden the horse's skin, surgical spirit can be rubbed daily into the areas most prone to galling.

POOR PERFORMANCE

A horse in pain cannot perform well. Instead of concentrating on our wishes, his mind can only focus on the pain he receives each time we move in the saddle or use the reins.

A common cause of the horse's not working well on the bit is pain in his mouth. Similarly, any discomfort from the saddle or girth can result in the horse's refusing to jump, or in resistance to perform certain movements. If we are not aware of the underlying problems, we may punish our horse unjustly, causing further resistance.

In all cases where the horse starts to behave abnormally, first suspect problems caused by tack. You might then consider having your horse's health checked by a professional. Only when these causes have been satisfactorily eliminated should you look towards the possibility that the horse is actually being naughty for no good reason.

Protecting tack from theft or damage is really a matter of common sense. To reduce the risks of damage, ensure that it is maintained and stored correctly. To protect it from thieves, ensure that it is well locked up when not in use. If you leave the tack room wide open and unattended when you go off to lunch you might as well issue the thief an invitation. While such preventative measures might take an extra few minutes, it pays to be cautious and conscientious.

You should also make sure your tack is fully insured; then, if it does get stolen, at least you will be able to replace it if it is not recovered.

PREVENTING THEFT

The number of tack thefts is increasing at an alarming rate and until recently people did not see the need to safeguard their tack. While it is true that marking tack does not stop the thief from taking it, it does enhance the chances of recovery, and it may also discourage the thief in the first place. Tack can be protected from theft in the following ways:

1. By indelible labelling.
2. By using metal stamps and punching a special number on all your tack. Many people use their post code as it is personal to them.
3. By using lockable tack racks.
4. By putting tack in lockable cabinets, fixed to the wall or floor.
5. By inserting a special identifying tag just inside the saddle stuffing.

In the event that a theft takes place, it is helpful if you are able to produce a comprehensive inventory of your tack, with all serial numbers and special distinguishing marks listed by each item. This will be necessary for the police and for the insurance company. It is also a good idea to have taken photographs of each separate item if necessary, so that there can be no doubt about ownership if an item is recovered. These will also help to value the tack, if there is any dispute regarding replacement value.

Dragging tack along the floor is careless and irresponsible.

Carelessness

Tack can be damaged in all sorts of ways, but most damage is caused by carelessness. Common damage and its cause include:

Damage   Tack being chewed by mice or scratched by cats.

Cause   Leaving tack on a saddle-horse or at a low level.

Damage   Tack being chewed by horse.

Cause   Tack left over stable door or in manger, or horse left unattended during tacking up.

Damage   Saddle knocked on to floor.

Cause   Saddle left over stable door with horse in stable. Saddle left over the back of a chair.

Damage   Scratched reins and martingales.

Cause   Tack being dragged along the floor while being carried.

Damage   Twisted tree.

Cause   Rider pulling heavily on cantle in order to mount. Rider unfit!

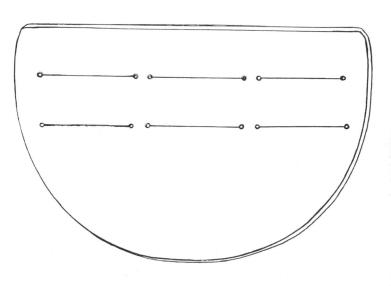

A girth safe will prevent the girth buckles from scratching the saddle flap.

If you leave your saddle over the stable door, while your horse is in the stable, you are asking for it to be knocked onto the floor . . .

. . . or for it to be chewed.

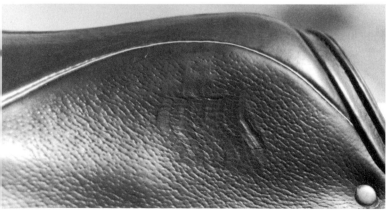

Bar (of mouth)   Area of toothless gum, on either side of the jaw, between the front teeth (incisors) and the back teeth (molars).

Bit   A device used in the horse's mouth, and to which the reins are attached, to enable the rider to control the horse's movements.

Boots   Used to protect a horse's legs when competing or travelling.

Breastplate   An item of tack anchored around the horse's neck and attached to the saddle to prevent it from slipping backwards.

Bridle   An item of tack fitted to the horse's head to provide the means of control over his movements.

Browband   The part of the bridle positioned on the forehead, under the forelock, and attached to the headpiece.

Bridle patch   The area behind the horse's ears where the headpiece of the bridle sits.

Cantle   The tip of the seat curve of the saddle, opposite the pommel.

Cat's hairs   The coarse hairs that grow out from between and around the jaw, not to be confused with the horse's whiskers.

Cheekpiece   The part of the bridle, attached to the headpiece, that supports the bit.

Cheek   The part of the bit that is visible and to which the reins are attached; equivalent to the bit rings of a snaffle.

Chin groove   The groove under the horse's lower jaw.

Conformation   The natural form and structure of the horse's body and limbs, which dictate the outline.

Curb-chain   The chain that is attached by hooks to a curb bit and sits in the jaw's chin groove.

Double bridle   A bridle that employs two bits.

Draw reins   A training aid: reins that run from the girth, up between the horse's forelegs, and through the bit rings to the rider's hands.

Ds   The small D-shaped rings on the front of a saddle or roller, to which other pieces of equipment can be attached.

Foalslip   A 'first' headcollar for a foal.

Flocking   The 'stuffing' in the panels of the saddle.

Gall (girth)   Hardened skin caused by an ill-fitting saddle and/or girth.

Girth   A thick strap used to secure the saddle on the horse's back.

Gullet   The channel between the panels of the underside of the saddle's seat.

Halter All-in-one headcollar and lead rope made from a single piece of strong cord.

Head carriage The manner in which a horse carries his head – high or low.

Headcollar An item of tack fitted on the horse's head and used to control him when he is not being ridden.

Headpiece The part of the bridle that rests on the top of the horse's head behind his ears.

Iron The part of the stirrup in which the rider's foot is placed.

Leaping head The lower, adjustable pommel on a side-saddle.

Lip-strap A thin leather strap, which attaches to the bit and runs through the curb-chain.

Lungeing cavesson An item of tack, fitted like a noseband, to which a lunge-rein is attached by a ring.

Martingale A device used to prevent the horse from throwing his head up.

Mouthpiece The part of the bit that is held in the horse's mouth.

Mullen (mouthpiece) Unjointed and slightly curved.

Neckstrap A strap fitted around the horse's neck to provide a hand-hold for the novice or nervous rider.

Noseband An item of tack fitted around the horse's nose, as part of the bridle, which helps to control his movements.

Numnah A piece of shaped padding used under the saddle.

Poll The top of the horse's head between the ears.

Poll guard An item fitted to the top of the horse's head between the ears to prevent injury in the event that the horse bashes his head on the roof of a horsebox while travelling.

Pommel The raised rounded part of the saddle, positioned above and slightly behind the withers.

Port A raised section in the centre of the bit's mouthpiece.

Reins The means of communication between the rider's hands and the bit.

Rein-stop Rubber or leather attachment to the reins to prevent the rings of a running martingale sliding too far towards the bit.

Ringworm A highly contagious fungal skin disease, characterized by rough, balding patches on the skin.

Roller A training aid: a wide strap, fitted like a girth and padded either side of the spine area, used in place of a saddle on a young or unschooled horse when lungeing; it has D-ring attachments to which other equipment, such as side-reins, can be attached.

Roundings Rolled piece of leather, mainly used on a Pelham bit, to permit the use of only a single rein.

Running reins A training aid: reins that run from either side of the girth, through the bit and back to the rider's hands; they encourage the horse to drop his nose.

Saddle An item of tack on which the rider sits when mounted.

Saddle cloth A cloth, used under the saddle like a numnah, to keep the saddle panels clean.

Saddle-horse A stand on which to rest a saddle for cleaning.

Setting-up The process of inserting and removing flocking from a saddle's panels in order to adjust the fit.

Side-reins A training aid: reins that connect the bit to the saddle or roller when lungeing; they are used to accustom the young horse to rein contact.

Slip-head A part of the bridle, acting like a second cheekpiece, to which a second bit – for example the bridoon of a double bridle – is attached.

Snaffle bridle A single bridle.

Stirrup An item of tack comprising the iron, in which the rider's foot is placed, and the leather strap (stirrup leather) by which the iron is attached to the saddle.

Surcingle A narrow webbing strap, like a girth, placed over the saddle to provide extra security.

Synthetic tack Tack made from a washable man-made material.

Tail guard A padded item that fits around the top of a horse's tail to prevent its sustaining damage if the horse rubs it.

Tongue groove A shallow port in a bit's mouthpiece.

Throat-lash Part of the bridle, an extension of the headpiece, which goes under the horse's throat and buckles on the near side of the horse's head.

Training aid Accessory used to help create the desired outline when schooling a horse.

Tree The 'skeleton' of the saddle. It is rigid or sprung, depending on the type of saddle.

Tushes The small pointed teeth that lie behind the incisors, and seen most commonly in male horses.

British Equestrian Trade Association
Wothersome Grange
Bramham
Nr Wetherby
West Yorkshire LS23 6LY
United Kingdom

The Pony Club
The British Equestrian Centre
Stoneleigh
Kenilworth
Warwickshire CV8 2LR
United Kingdom

The British Horse Society
(as for Pony Club)

Saddlers' Company
40 Gutter Lane
London EC2V 6BR
United Kingdom

The Side-Saddle Association
Highbury House
19 High Street
Welford
Northampton NN6 7HT
United Kingdom

Society of Master Saddlers
Kettles Farm
Mickfield
Stowmarket
Suffolk IP14 6BY
United Kingdom

Worshipful Company of Loriners
50 Cheyne Avenue
London E18 2DR
United Kingdom

American Horse Shows Association Inc.
220 East 42nd Street
4th Floor
New York
NY 10017-5806
USA

National Snaffle Bit Association
1513 Cleveland Avenue
#109 B
East Point
GA 30344
USA

The International Side-Saddle Organization
P.O. Box 4076
Mount Holly
New Jersey 08060
USA

United States Professional Horseman's Association Inc.
4059 Ironworks Pike
Lexington
KY 40511
USA

Western and English Manufacturers Association
789 Sherman Street
#160
Denver
CO 80203
USA

Western/English Retailers of America
2011 Eye Street
NW #600
Washington DC 20006
USA

British Horse Society, *Manual of Horsemanship,* Threshold Books (1993)

Saddlery, Threshold Books (1991)

Hartley Edwards, Elwyn, *Saddlery,* J A Allen (1992)

Bitting, J A Allen (1990)

The Saddle, J A Allen (1990)

Training Aids, J A Allen (1990)

Townley, Audrey, *The Natural Horse,* The Crowood Press, (1993)

Tuke, Diana, *Bit by Bit,* J A Allen (1965)

McBane, Susan, *The Illustrated Guide to Horse Tack,* David & Charles (1992)